SURVIVAL TIPS
for WORKING MOMS

SURVIVAL TIPS
for WORKING MOMS

297 REAL Tips *from* REAL Moms

Linda Goodman Pillsbury

Illustrated by Barry Wetmore

Perspective Publishing
Los Angeles

Library of Congress Catalog Card Number 93-087732
ISBN 0-9622036-5-3

Published by Perspective Publishing, Inc.
2528 Sleepy Hollow Dr. #A; Glendale, CA 91206
800-330-5851; 818-502-1270; fax 818-502-1272
books@familyhelp.com
www.familyhelp.com

Additional copies of this book may be ordered by calling toll free
1-800-330-5851, or by sending $14.95 ($10.95 + $4 shipping) to the above
address. CA residents add 8.25% sales tax ($.90). Discounts available for
quantity orders. Bookstores, please call LPC Group at 1-800-626-4330.

Publisher's Cataloging-in-Publication Data

Pillsbury, Linda G.

    Survival tips for working moms : 297 real tips from real moms :
food, clothes, morning, evening, errands, chores, homework,
grown-up time & more / Linda Goodman Pillsbury ; illustrated by
Barry Wetmore
    p. cm.
    Includes bibliographical references
    ISBN 0-9622036-5-3
    1. Working mothers—Life skills guides. 2. Parenting. 3. Children
of working mothers. I. Title.

HQ759.48.P55 1994
646.7'00852

    QBI93-22658

Illustrations by Barry Wetmore
Back cover photo by Sam Pillsbury
Printed in the United States of America
Third Printing: 2000

acknowledgement

I would like to thank all those moms and a few dads who contributed to this book. As we said on the cover, these are real tips, and I am grateful for everyone's willingness to share. I learned so much. So, thank you to:

Judy Alder

Della Bahan

Wendy Nevett Bazil

Marlene Benz

Anne Broussard

Marie Campbell

Pat Chambers

Holly Ciotti

Jennie Cook

Lynn Dannhausen

Lesley Dewing

Janet Elkins

Nan Freitas

Lynn Foerster

Chris Jansen Gillum

Diane A. Goodman

Pat Griffith

Margaret Paticopoulous Hazapis

Judith Head

Markrid Izquierdo

Micheline Jedrey

Lois Jensen

Susan Kaplan

Sheila Kraus

Cally Lau

Susan Cannon Lapekas

Valerie Levett

Gina Lobaco

Joanne Loeb

Therese Maynard

Joy McCallum

Liz McHale

Toni Miller

Marilyn Morrison

Micki Nevett

Lolita Parker

Adeles Pickar

Hope Pillsbury

Kate Pillsbury

Patti Pinto

Dale Raisig

Nancy Robertson

Robin Robinson

Nancy Rosen

Lee Rothman

Lisa Sachs

Faith Sand

Patricia Satoh

Denise Seider

Sandy Sloane

Dale Sogge

Emily Smythe

Penny Sonnenschein

Monica Villegas

Jayne Wallace

Barry Wetmore

Cynthia Whitham

Jane Winer

Connie Woodhead

Pansy Yee

Contents

Introduction

WHEN MY FRIEND, LESLEY, DECIDED to go back to work, she asked me for suggestions and commented that she didn't want to reinvent the wheel. She thought that her working friends probably had a few shortcuts and had figured out how to balance conflicting obligations. The more I thought about her questions, the more I realized that we all could use a few tips. So I started asking friends and acquaintances what works for them. This book is made up of real tips from real people.

The biggest issue facing working moms is establishing priorities. Since there are so many things that need doing and not enough time in the day, we have to decide what is most important. When I was in college, my friends and I assumed we could have it all–highpowered career, good marriage, kids, and time for ourselves. The reality, of course, is quite different. We had no idea just how much work having a a family is. We really do have to decide to let the housework slide in order to spend some time with the kids, to work a little less to see our husbands, or to work more and have no time for our own interests. I think the first hurdle is to realize you can't do everything—and not feel guilty about it. Letting go of the guilt is hard, but face it, worrying and feeling guilty actually take time and energy. Wouldn't you rather use that time to read a book or sleep? The next thing is to learn how to delegate. Get other family members to share home responsibilities. Delegate more at work (I don't mean slack off, but share some responsibility).

As you flip through you will notice that tips often contradict other tips. What works in one family often does not work in another. What I have tried to do is offer many suggestions on the issues that overwhelm us all. This is not meant to be an all-inclusive plan. Use what you need. I have taken home many of these tips and tried them out on my own family. They have helped us. I suggest, though, to start small. Some of the tips require a lot of effort. Try some of the easy ones first.

1 ▪ Getting Started

LOOK OVER THE FOLLOWING LIST and jot down who in your family is responsible for getting it done. If more than one person does the chore, put that down. Add any chores or responsibilities not included. Then look at your list carefully. If you are doing almost everything yourself, it is time to start dividing jobs among family members (or get some outside help). Admittedly, if you are a single mom with very young children, you *are* responsible for almost everything. But if you have a partner or your kids are out of diapers, everyone can pitch in. Have a family meeting to divide up responsibilities.

A typical day
Get the children up
Get them dressed
Breakfast
Brush teeth
Brush hair
Pack backpack/diaper bag
Drive to school/daycare
Pick up from school/daycare
Drive and pick up from lessons & activities
Supervise homework
Fix dinner
Set table
Clear table
Wash dishes
Clean table
Sweep floor
Supervise bathtime
PJ's
Pick out clothes for next day
Brush teeth
Read stories
Lights out
Enforce bedtime

Sick kids
Stay home
Take to doctor
Rearrange other kids' plans
Arrange other care

Cleaning
Living room
   straighten
   vacuum
   clean furniture
Dining room
   straighten
   vacuum
   clean furniture
Kitchen
   mop floor
   run dishwasher
   empty dishwasher
   clean sink and counters
Family room
   put away toys
   vacuum
Bathroom(s)
   clean sink
   toilet
   tub/shower
   mop floor
Kids' rooms
   make bed
   pick up toys
   vacuum
Your room
   make bed
   straighten
   vacuum
Empty wastebaskets

Laundry
Put clothes in hamper
Empty hamper
Change towels
Change sheets
   kids beds
   your bed
Wash clothes
Sort clothes
Put away clothes

Groceries
Make shopping list
Buy groceries
Unload from car
Put away groceries

Outside
Mow lawn
Water lawn
Rake leaves
Prune trees & bushes
Compost heap
Sweep front porch
Sweep patio or deck
Shovel steps
Shovel driveway
Put garbage out

Errands
Drycleaners
Bank
Drugstore
School supplies
Buy kids' clothes
Buy birthday presents
Doctor's appointments

Car(s)
Gas
Maintenance
Carwash

Organization
Book babysitters
Arrange playdates
Plan parties
Research lessons, etc.

School
Parent meetings
Arrange teacher conferences
Attend teacher conferences
Communicate with teacher
Fulfill "volunteer" obligations

2 ∎
Basics

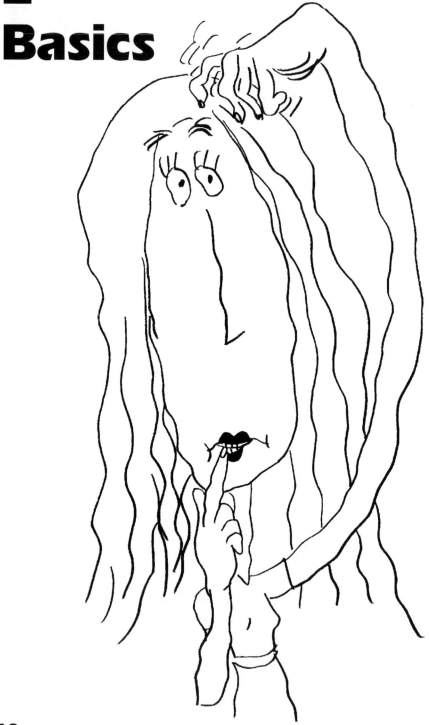

WHERE SHOULD WE START? We all have so much to do, so many people to coordinate, and so little time to stop and think. Many of these suggestions will seem obvious, but I find that in zooming from one thing to the next, it is easy to lose sight of the basics. We forget how much we really love and enjoy the children despite their demands and tantrums. We forget how much we care about work when there is simply not time to do it well and manage the family. We are overwhelmed by all that needs doing. So let's just start.

1. Have a good sense of humor.

(And retain it practically at all costs.)

2. Keep expectations realistic.

3. Take it one day at a time.

As a new mom, Wendy has learned that planning ahead helps a great deal, but worrying ahead doesn't help. Just worry about what has to be done today.

4. A close family is more important than a clean house.

Lee suggests reminding yourself at least once a week of why you had children, and how much you love them. Make a little time to just be with them.

5. Listen to your kids.

Hear their joys and pains and struggles to grow. Adele suggests that if you cannot be available when they want to talk to you, set aside a special time that you both agree to.

6. Compromise.

Don't feel compelled to meet everyone else's standards. Buy a dessert for a party; don't drive yourself crazy making one. Connie learned this from the friend that inspired her to have children. The friend chose not to breastfeed when the social pressure to do so was enormous. Decide for yourself what is *really* important to *you*.

7. Don't punish yourself.

Judy warns not to "ground" your child unless you are prepared to stay home and be "grounded" yourself. It only took Liz once to realize that taking away Saturday morning cartoons (and her sleep-in time) was worse for her than for the kids.

8. Have a group of three or four people who can help you out on very short notice.

Janet has a small group of other parents whom she can call to pick up her kids, etc. She, of course, pitches in when they need her. This has made a huge difference.

9. Make a friend whose children are a few years older than your children.

When you need advice you have someone to call. Joy has found her friend's help and advice invaluable because invariably the friend's older children have already lived through whatever problem Joy and her kids are facing.

10. Keep the diaper bag packed and ready either in the car or by the door.

Include extra clothes, snacks (for you, too) and a few toys in addition to diapers, wipes, plastic bags.

11. Keep a bag packed for older children, too.

For her three-year-old, Nancy includes extra clothes (shirt, pants, underwear, socks), sunscreen, visor, sunglasses, crackers, raisins, juice boxes, plastic bags (for accidents), and baby wipes. Napkins and tissues are also good to have along. Sheila finds a packed bag helpful even for six and seven-year-olds.

12. Keep a stash of supplies in your car or trunk.

Jane has snacks, drinks and Tylenol at all times. Marilyn keeps a package of wet wipes in the car. They are great for sticky hands and faces even for older children and grown-ups. She also keeps a couple of air sickness bags from the airlines in the car. You never know when someone may need one. Band-aids and extra tissues are also on hand in her purse as well as in the car. These can all be stored in a plastic crate or a small zip-up duffel.

13. Keep a list of everything you need for outings.

Post it next to the door so you can check as you leave. If you go on lots of different outings like the beach, hiking, movies, you can have several different lists all typed up clearly on a sheet by the door.

14. Learn a bit about child development.

One of the most important things for Jane is having an idea of what she can expect her child to be like and what she can expect him to do at every age. Obviously, children are different, but she finds that knowing something about child development—ie. 5-year-olds probably *can* dress themselves and six-year-olds probably will have a hard time making up their minds, really helps her deal with her son. For this information, Jane turns to the Ames & Ilg books, *Your Five Year Old: Sunny and Serene*, etc.

15. When your children are older, discuss their plans with them.

Rather than have a set curfew, Judy suggests that before they go out, ask the kids where they are going, who they are going with, and what time they will be back. Make sure you both agree that it's okay. When discussing changes parents should feel free to disagree. (Simply say "I don't feel comfortable with ...") If for any reason they can't make it back on time or their plans change they must call and discuss it. You will find that the kids are probably more conservative with their limits than you would be. Always remember, though, that you are the parent and make the final decisions.

3.
Communication & Organization

MOST PEOPLE SAY they love their families. When I was younger I was certain that the only ingredient that counted in a marriage was love—if you loved each other everything would work out. I still think that's mostly true, but it takes a big commitment to communication and organization to set up a system for your family that runs smoothly. Some people are highly organized and like to map out everything; others are more comfortable with flexibility. Many of the women I talked to lamented that they were not as organized as they should be. Some constantly compare themselves to the mythical "Super Mom." The truth is that there is no organizational standard to which we must measure up. We all do our best to find a way to make things work for our own particular families. The point of these suggestions is not to make you feel guilty that you are not organized enough, but to share ideas that work for some people.

Keeping track

16. Make lists to remind yourself.

Lynn reports that if she makes a list, less slips through the cracks. She still "messes up" but a lot less than she used to.

17. Use a calendar.

Lesley finds that one master calendar for everyone works well. You write in everyone's appointments and activities and put it up where everyone can refer to it. Emily does this, too, but even includes things like washing the kids' hair and regular chores. She says the kids like knowing what is going to happen, and are more responsible if they know what to expect. Because she puts so much detail on the family calendar, Emily goes to the stationery store and buys one of those big ones with lots of room to write. Susan uses a big one that wipes off with a cloth. Each family member is assigned a different color marker. This really helps Susan and her husband see at a glance who is doing what and that the pickups are taken care of. Lynn keeps one family calendar on the wall at home, one on her desk at work and one in her purse. Every week she updates all of them so she knows who needs to be where. Diane likes to keep an engagement calendar next to the telephone so she can answer requests to do something at a glance.

18. Make up your own weekly master schedule.

Penny finds that writing down the regular activities can be repetitive so she has drawn up a weekly master schedule with all the regular things on it like hours of nursery school, gym class... She puts all the things for both kids on it and then copies it and leaves a copy out all the time so she or the babysitter can add play dates, doctor's appointments, and all the extras. Therese does the same, changing the master schedule by season, as the school and sports schedules change. She also makes sure her husband has a copy. When she travels for work, it is much easier for everyone to remember all the things that need to be coordinated.

19. Buy a large dry erase board and hang it in the kitchen or hallway near your calendar and telephone.

Marilyn divides hers into sections for the various committees she's on, plus sections for the grocery list and general things to do. You can use different colored pens to assign priority, or indicate different family member's information. When the job is done, just erase the entry. It gives a great sense of completion!

20. Have a set place for notes from school.

Do you often feel that you miss the notes that come home from school? That your child can't remember what he was supposed to give you or tell you? Pat has a solution. Five-year-old Taylor made a mailbox at home. He decorated a shoebox and found a conspicuous place to put it (on the dining room table). When he comes home he puts any notes or book orders or other communication from school in the "mailbox." He can also put library books in his "mailbox" and then they are no longer his responsibility. This way Pat sees all the notes without rifling through Taylor's backpack, pockets, and lunch box.

21. Make home mailboxes for everyone.

The mailbox has been working well for Pat, but she even has some improvement suggestions. Have mailboxes for everyone in the house. Put in phone messages, notes, reminders, invitations, notes home from school, etc. Have everyone check their box when arriving home. This works especially well for older children and teens whose erratic activity schedules make them hard to catch. It also cuts down on having notes all over the house—on the refrigerator, by the phone (which phone?), etc.

22. Keep library books on a separate shelf.

It is easy to gather them up on library day and cuts down on lost and overdue books.

23. Call your spouse every day just before you leave work.

This helps Dale be sure about who's picking up the kids and that he can get there on time. It saves day care penalties. You can also find out if there is something you need to pick up on the way home.

Talking things over

24. Don't get locked in.
Reassess at least every few months. If something isn't working, sit down and figure out a solution, and change what you are doing. Micki has found that periodic fine tuning is the only way to approach all the juggling.

25. Try a family meeting.
When things aren't working the way you want, sit down with the whole family, outline the problems and ask for help in coming up with solutions that will help everyone.

26. Tell your partner about work commitments.
If you both travel for work, tell each other as soon as you know you may have to be away. Wendy says this avoids last minute panic as well as deciding whose trip is more important.

27. Schedule working lunches with your husband.
Marilyn and her husband use the time to discuss household business like planning vacations, household repairs, the kids' extracurricular activities or problems, making holiday gift lists, etc. They have an agenda and bring their calendars and any brochures or other information. It works great because they can talk about important things when they are not too tired and they don't have to pay a babysitter to have a little space while they discuss things.

28. Have a nagging policy and stick to it.

If the kids bug her repeatedly about anything, Judy has a policy response, "If you want an answer now, the answer is NO." This has cut nagging way down.

29. Give yourself space to respond to requests.

We are bombarded with requests from the kids, committees, schools, etc. Instead of deciding on the spot and making a decision you might regret, Dale suggests saying "Let me get back to you." This relieves the pressure and allows you to decide in peace. Of course, you do need to decide and get back to the person. Della, however, recommends avoiding "maybe." It just prolongs the agony of decisions (and increases the begging and whining).

Family rules

30. Make the family rules clear and stick to them.

Susan and her husband sit down with their son, Benjamin, every year around his birthday and establish (or re-establish) Rules and Consequences. Rules have to be in the child's language so he or she can understand them, and consequences have to be important to the child. Some of the rules are basic, like no lying or hurting other people or beings, and some are specific to what is going on at a particular time, like homework must be done as soon as you come home. At this family conference, Benjamin participates in developing the consequences, so he knows exactly what he's getting in for when he breaks a rule. The rules and consequences are posted so they can be referred to if a problem arises.

31. Try fines for breaking family rules.

Therese found that she was tired of taking privileges away, which seemed to punish the babysitter or other family members more than the child herself. So she borrowed from real life. Family rules are posted in the hall on a laminated sheet. If rules are broken, the children (or parents) pay a fine. Many families do not want to use fines as punishments but it is working for Therese.

32. Praise good behavior more and scold less.
Kate reminds us that it really pays off.

Saving time

33. Pack the diaper bag the night before with everything but the perishables.

If you want to be super organized you can stick it in the car so you don't have to balance the baby, the briefcase and the diaperbag.

34. Make the kids pack their backpacks the night before.

That's the time to make sure they remember homework, a sweatshirt, etc. Put the backpacks by the door.

35. Keep your desk organized both at home and at work.

Kate read that the average person spends three hours a week looking for things on her or his desk.

36. Teach your children to answer the telephone.

It can give you a few extra minutes and teaches them a useful skill.

4■
Food

I AM ALWAYS AMAZED at how much time and effort food takes. Preparing gourmet meals is not even the issue. Just having three healthy meals a day, every day, for everyone in the family, takes major time. I like to cook for company, I like to bake, and I love to sit around eating hors d'oeuvres with family and friends, but I get sick of being responsible for the everyday food preparation that you can't skip. My best suggestion, of course, is to not be responsible for it all. Divide the responsibilities up with your partner and children. I realize that this is easier said than done, but even partners with a long history of not helping can change (or be forced to change). Before we had children, my husband and I used to eat at seven o'clock. Then I got a new job which kept me at work later. I got home at seven and my husband wanted dinner right away. I finally gave him a choice: "Either I cook dinner and we eat at 7:30 or you cook dinner and we eat at seven." He chose to learn how to cook. For about a month I had to leave a list of what was for dinner and how to cook it, but after that he figured it out, and for the three-and-a-half years I had that job, I had the same good deal which many men have—I walked in and dinner was on the table. Now we periodically renegotiate dinner responsibilities. He is not comfortable with "whoever gets home first starts dinner." He would rather have set days that are his responsibility. Besides not having to cook dinner on those days, I don't have to field any complaints about it. If the kids have a problem, I refer them to their father. This may not be practical for many families, and even if it is, some of the following suggestions can help save you time.

Breakfast

37. If you drink coffee, buy a programmable coffeemaker.

You turn it on the night before and the coffee is ready in the morning. If that is too sophisticated (and they really are not hard to use), Cynthia, who is bleary without her morning caffeine, recommends having your coffeemaker all set so you can stagger into the kitchen and turn it on as soon as you wake up. Then, by the time you are showered and dressed your coffee will be ready.

38. If you are in a rush, give your child breakfast in the car on the way to daycare.

Hope recommends Cheerios for toddlers because they take a long time to eat and are not too messy. Either buy deep bowls for this, or better yet, put them in a plastic container with a top so if your child doesn't finish them in the morning they will be in the car waiting on the way home. For older children, pack something extra in their lunch boxes so they can choose something on the way.

39. Make everyone in the family responsible for his own breakfast.

Have bowls, spoons, and cereal at kid level. Also have bread and toaster ready. For younger children have the milk poured into a little container so they can pour their own. You can even pour the cereal into a bowl the night before and leave it on the table covered with a plate. While preschoolers will need some help, they can do a lot on their own. One day I stopped by my daughter's preschool at snacktime and all the four-year-olds were pouring their own milk and water from small plastic containers. If they can do it at school they can do it at home.

40. **If you make pancakes (on the weekends)
double the recipe and freeze the extra.**
They heat up quickly in the microwave.

41. Allow only healthy cereal for breakfast.

Connie stopped the demand for sugary cereals by telling the kids they could buy them for dessert but not breakfast. Judy makes the kids read the labels on the cereals at the store, and does not allow any without 2 grams of protein per serving.

Lunch

42. Pack lunches the night before.

Isn't packing lunches the worst? (or almost?) Lots of moms have suggested packing lunches the night before, but I never figured out how to keep the wax bags from getting mushy or the sandwiches from drying out. Well now I know. Get a bunch of little plastic containers. Carrots and sliced apples can be fixed the night before and put in a container in the refrigerator. Pretzels, cookies, etc. can go in another mini-container and straight into the lunch box. The sandwich can also be put in a plastic sandwich container and stored perfectly well overnight. Just gather all the little containers in the morning.

43. Buy several lunchboxes or cloth lunch bags.

Washing out the lunchbox and then drying it before you can start packing the next day's lunch can really slow you down. If you've got several, there's always a clean one ready. I prefer the cloth lunch bags because they go in the wash and they don't take up much room in a drawer.

44. Make life easy for yourself.

If your kids like peanut butter and jelly that's great. If they'll eat cold cuts, spend a little extra if you can and buy sliced meat for easy sandwiches. If they like frozen vegetables, throw some in the lunch box; they'll be warm and edible by lunch time. Don't feel you have to be a supermom and make homemade tuna or egg salad every day. Lots of kids like hotdogs for lunch. One minute in the microwave, slap on a bun and it's okay for the lunchbox (maybe not every day, but sometimes). Leftovers are also great for lunch. While you are cleaning up from dinner, stick the extra in a lunch container.

45. Keep a container full of carrots sticks and celery in the refrigerator.

On the weekend, peel and cut a whole bag of carrots and bunch of celery, put them in the refrigerator with water, and they are ready for school lunches. Even easier, try buying the precut carrot and celery sticks.

46. Cook ahead for toddler lunches.

Susan cooks about two adult servings of frozen vegetables and starch (plain spagetti, macaroni, etc.) on Sunday, and puts some in her toddler's lunch everyday.

47. Sit down with your child and make a list of what she will eat for lunch.

Then you can choose from the list when you make the lunch. For Lois, this saves the "I don't know what I want today" broken record and fighting. If your child gets sick of tuna every day, she can take it off the list for a while. If you post the list, your child can add to it as well as delete from it.

48. Teach the children to pack their own lunches.

The earlier they become responsible for it, the less you have to do. My eight-year-old, Leah, can make her lunch. She doesn't like to be responsible for it every day (who does?). Our challenge is to work her up to full responsibility. We have found that if we set aside a day (or days) it works well, ie. "every Thursday you do your own lunch," and work up from there.

49. Make it easy for your child to pack lunch.

Jordan has made her own lunch since she was about eight. She has her own box in the pantry and her own drawer in the refrigerator for her lunch food. She goes with her mom to the market and chooses what she wants for the week. This eliminates the "there's nothing in the house" refrain. Jordan always has what she wants and her parents don't have to make her lunch. (There are rules for sweets—Jordan can pack one pudding or two cookies in addition to a healthy lunch. The rules are clear and Jordan follows them.)

50. Buy the school lunches.

Anne has found that it saves a lot of time and is cheaper than packing their own. She can pay for the whole year in advance and doesn't have to worry about having change in the morning. Then occasionally packing a special lunch is fun.

Dinner

51. Plan ahead.

When I was growing up, my mother planned out a weekly menu, did the shopping and stuck to it. I do not know anyone quite that organized, but it does help dinner run more smoothly. You don't have to think about what's for dinner, and the food is all there. Several friends have told me that the key is knowing what is for dinner by 9 or 10 o'clock the night before. Then you have a chance to take something out of the freezer or even get the crock pot ready.

52. Eat early.

That sounds ridiculous when you are working, hassled and tired, but when we manage to eat at 5:30, everyone is more cheerful and there is more useful time afterwards. Before kids we had a 7 pm dinnertime but several of my more experienced friends have suggested 5:30 and I have to admit it makes a big difference. The key, of course, is planning ahead what you will have for dinner, and having plenty of canned soup on hand to get started.

53. Keep it simple.

With three children and her own catering business, Jennie has a lot of good suggestions about dinners. She suggests spending the extra money on "quick cook" meats like boneless chicken and precut beef. Try precut fresh vegetables. Sautee lots of diced carrots onions, and celery and add it to any recipe for increased flavor. Buy a rice cooker and then use it. It only takes two things to make a good meal, for example—pasta and broccoli, rice and vegetables, chicken and salad. Center the meal around the carbohydrates (which the kids like) and it is easier to plan. Check the women's magazines at the checkout counter for new fast ideas.

54. Very quick and easy is OKAY.

Judy reminds us that it is okay to have waffles for dinner. When you are tired fix something quick and easy. Scrambled eggs are a favorite in our house for a quick, hot dinner.

55. Try hors d'oeuvres.

Don't you hate that screeching while you are trying to fix dinner and would rather be resting and reading the paper? Give the kids something to eat right away. Nothing fancy, just cut up some cheese and apples. Put out some salami, and the kids quiet down. Or heat up some soup for while they are waiting. Anne finds that giving the kids fruit and cheese allows them to eat late and have a more relaxing family dinner.

56. Serve vegetables first.

When kids are hungry they are less picky. Chris finds they will devour broccoli while waiting for the main course.

57. Let the kids watch a video while you fix dinner.

On those nights when she is really tired, Hope comes home from work and lets her toddler watch a video while she makes dinner. "Sometimes I even eat dinner first!"

58. Let your kids choose and plan dinner—in exchange for helping prepare it.

This is one that has to be done ahead of time (ie. before the marketing) or you are in for an evening of screeching over not having what she wants. Eight-year-old Leah is much more enthusiastic about what she chooses, and she really can help or even prepare the meal totally herself—if she's not too tired.

59. Use your crock pot a lot.

Lesley has adapted many of her family's favorite dinners for the crock pot. If you prepare it the night before, you just have to turn it on in the morning and dinner is ready when you get home.

60. Go out for fast food occasionally or bring take-out food in.

It might seem obvious, but I was talking to some moms and one commented that how come the nights dad was responsible for dinner they often went out for fast food, but she never did because they couldn't afford it? Split the fast-food budget more equitably so you get a break, too.

61. Find a babysitter who can cook.

This saves Lisa's marriage. She can come home from work and not have to either fix dinner or negotiate with her husband to fix it. If you have in-home child care, you might want to include fixing dinner as part of the job.

62. Cook in batches and freeze the extra.

Micki suggests that if you are cooking, just make double and freeze the rest.

63. Cook a big pot of hearty soup on Sunday.

Chris has soup ready all week long for supper or snacks (or even in a thermos in the lunchbox).

64. Cook for the week on the weekend.

On Sunday Pansy cooks two casseroles, each large enough to last two nights. If she finds herself caught in the middle of the week without dinner for the next night, as soon as dinner is over, she makes it for the following night.

65. Cook a roast once a week.

Diane finds the leftovers make easy dinners and lunches. She also keeps a large bowl of jello, rice pudding, custard or stewed fruit in the refrigerator so dessert is always ready.

Other food things

66. Rent an electric breast pump.

Lots of moms report it is quicker and easier. Some large employers even have electric breast pumps to lend out to their employees. Nancy suggests that if you are pumping at work, bring plastic

bottles (not the disposable ones) to work to pump into. If you don't have an accessible refrigerator at work, you can bring one of those small individual coolers to store the milk in.

67. Freeze breast milk in individual plastic bottle liners.

You can bring them to child care frozen and the provider can warm them up as needed.

68. Keep a food mill in your diaper bag if your baby is eating solids.

Wherever you go, the baby can eat what you eat.

69. Mix formula when you need it.

If you want warm milk for the baby and will be gone all day, Hope suggests mixing up the formula with half the amount of water and keeping that in a little cooler. Bring along a separate thermos of warm water and mix it up whenever you need it. Our pediatrician said to bring along the powdered formula and just mix it with tap water—it doesn't need to be warm.

70. Keep your freezer and pantry well stocked.

Then at least you don't have to run out to the market.

71. Keep some box juices in the freezer .

Connie likes to be prepared for those last minute announcements that there is a field trip the next day.

72. Make it easy for the kids to help themselves.

If you want your kids to cook more and get more things for themselves (releasing you from your role as waitress), rearrange your kitchen to make things accessible. Therese has moved all the dishes to a lower cabinet. Joanne has filled a drawer with plastic plates and cups.

73. Buy food that is easy to prepare.

Therese has found that the kids will fix it themselves.

74. Plan an evening snack.

If you eat dinner early, the kids may want a snack before bed. Adele suggests having them in their pajamas and using this as a transition time between the day's activities and bedtime.

75. Put the recipes you like on index cards.

Penny finds that having all the recipes together and easily accessible cuts down the time spent searching for a recipe. It is also easy to pull a recipe and leave it out for someone else to cook.

76. Uses a 3-ring notebook with photo album pages to store recipes cut out of magazines or the newspaper.

For Marilyn it beats having all those scraps of paper hanging around, and the recipes stay clean while she cooks.

5 ■
Clothes

THE BOTTOM LINE IS that everyone has to wear clothes every day. It is easier if you have enough clothes so you don't have to worry about doing the laundry during the week after work. Some people insist on their children wearing neat matching outfits. Others are comfortable with obviously well-used mismatched play clothes. As long as clothes start out clean, I generally do not care what my children wear (as long as they are dressed) but I have often wondered if people think my kids are orphans. Seriously, though, whatever you are comfortable with is fine. If you find it stressful for your children to live up to your standards, consider relaxing them and saving the ironing for special occasions. The same is true for your own clothes. Obviously you need to dress appropriately for work, but think about easy-care clothes or sending work clothes to the dry cleaners.

Buying

77. Limit sock colors.
Doesn't it drive you crazy when you finish sorting the laundry and there are half a dozen different colored singles?

78. Buy ONLY easy to maintain clothes.
Lesley skips the things that must be ironed or washed separately (especially for the kids).

79. Buy children's clothes that absolutely mix and match.
No matter what the top is, the bottom goes. Susan says to forget the very adorable light colored items. They look terrible after one or two wearings. Also she finds that solid colors (particularly for tops) show stains much sooner than patterns. Lynn buys all the clothes with color themes that look good together so they all mix and match. Kate, however, recommends buying a lot of solids and a lot of white shirts so it is easy to find clothing that matches. Monica thinks black is a great color for kids—it goes with everything and doesn't show the dirt. Different colors work for different people, but the point is to make picking out clothes easy for your kids and yourself.

80. Uses the color theme idea for your own work wardrobe.
Gina buys several skirts that look good with the same blazer and blouses that go with several outfits.

81. Uses a purse with a long shoulder strap.
Toni drapes it across her body, leaving both hands free to hold the children's hands.

82. Go shopping without the kids.
Marilyn takes along a shirt and a pair of pants to help judge what size to buy.

83. Have a plan for shopping with older kids.

As the children get older and they have definite ideas about clothes, it becomes almost impossible to shop without them. When Judy takes her daughters shopping and they see something they "have to have" but she doesn't want to buy, she offers them the opportunity to pay for half of it. Often they decide they don't really *need* it.

84. Try a clothing allowance.

Some families put their older children on a clothing allowance and they learn to budget their money and choose wisely. This can build good money habits, or it can cause anxiety if a child isn't ready. Susan suggests a variation of this—buy their basic wardrobe, but have them pay for anything trendy. This, of course, requires you to define what is basic. It might end up being a definition that includes price as well as what the item is. For example, you might be willing to spend $35 for sneakers, but anything over that comes out of the child's money.

85. Buy clothes by mail order.

It saves trips to the store.

86. Buy clothes at consignment (second hand, resale, almost new) shops for you and the children.

It saves money and you can get some fabulous buys. (Consignment shops carry higher quality merchandise than thrift stores).

Dressing

87. Pick out clothes the night before.

Whether you are doing the choosing, or your child, it saves a lot of time and aggravation to have the clothes all picked out. Nancy suggests that if you pick out the clothes you can pick out two outfits and let your child choose in the morning.

88. Give your kids breakfast in their pajamas.

If they spill you don't have to change their clothes. Kate finds that this saves her a lot of time and aggravation. Other moms like to have their kids dressed and ready before breakfast; it just depends which is more of a problem for you: getting them dressed or keeping their clothes clean.

89. Let the children wear whatever they want (and don't worry about matching clothes).

When they are small, who really cares what they wear? Connie has found it is not too long before they become fashion conscious and pick out clothes that match all on their own. Therese also lets the kids wear what they want as long as their clothes are weather appropriate. She's found that by being tolerant on a daily basis it is easier to gain their cooperation on those few occasions when what they wear is important.

90. Push for a school uniform.

Nancy reports that when her twelve-year-old switched to a school with a uniform, at least 45 minutes a day was saved and it made everyone's morning a lot easier. If your school (some public as well as private schools have uniforms) is considering adopting a uniform, push it. Or suggest it at the next parent meeting.

91. Pick out your own clothes the night before.

It saves time and thinking.

92. Only dress *yourself* once a day.

If she's going out after work, Hope wears something that will go both places so she doesn't have to change. Diane finds suits particularly useful if she has an after work event. She can bring an extra blouse and change in the ladies room.

93. If you hate wearing your work clothes around afterwards, bring your own play clothes in the car.

Lee likes to relax after work, so she often brings a set of casual clothes and changes before she picks up her daughter at school.

Washing

94. Spray baby clothes with stain remover before you throw them in the hamper.

Susan finds it makes washing them a lot easier.

95. When sorting the laundry, bundle outfits in rubberbands (saved from all those junk flyers).

Put together shirt, pants and socks all in one rubber band. When your child chooses he will pick whole outfits and has everything needed. Cynthia started this when her kids were babies, to save her from searching for the matching socks. It is especially useful for toddlers; they still have a choice but there are fewer decisions and dressing goes more quickly.

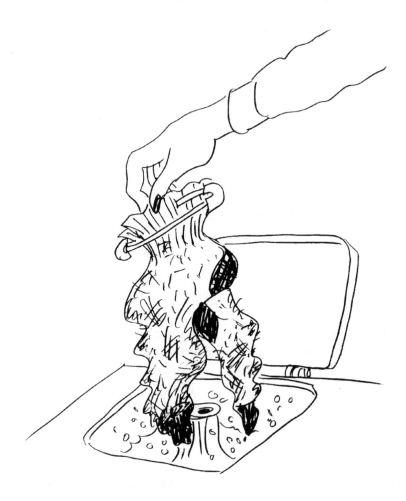

96. Use a safety pin to pin socks together right after the kids take them off, before throwing them in the hamper.

If different kids have similar socks, use different colored diaper pins, one color for each child. With two sons close in age, this has saved Holly a lot of mix-ups and sorting. Diane suggests washing socks in a zippered mesh bag. If each child has her own bag, their socks won't get lost or mixed up.

97. Teach your older children to do their own laundry.

Does it annoy you that your older children seem to change outfits three times a day? Robin decided that they should do their own laundry. It only took one or two weeks of chaos before they learned to do it themselves and she didn't have to worry about their clothes.

6 ∎
Morning

IT'S A TOSS-UP, WHICH IS TOUGHER, morning or evening. Getting everyone up and ready, out the door and to school and work on time can be exhausting. It's hard enough when the kids cooperate, but when they lounge around in bed, refuse to get dressed, whine about

their clothes, and demand that I fix their breakfast, it makes me feel like trading it all in (or literally walking out the door without them). There are obviously no easy answers, but changing your routine even a little bit can often help enormously.

Getting up

98. Juggle baby's early wake-ups with your partner.

Give each other a break when one is not as sleepy or as stressed from work.

99. Try morning "giggle time."

Marlene finds it helps get the kids up cheerfully. She wakes them up fifteen minutes early to tickle, giggle, and snuggle together with her.

100. Buy your kids an alarm clock.

It sounds simple or maybe too impersonal, but if your kids are resisting your efforts at waking them up, try an alarm clock or clock radio. They can't be mad at you when the "clock" wakes them up. This also works with kids who get up too early. You can say, "Don't get out of your room until the alarm or clock radio goes off."

Getting ready

101. Shower and dress yourself (in peace) before you wake the kids up.

Sandy figures that once the kids are up she has no time for herself, and if she wants to look nice for work (which she does) the only way is to take care of herself first.

102. Tell your children it is their responsibility to dress themselves (as soon as they are able).

Let them know that if they don't they will go to school in their pajamas. Once to school in PJ's is usually enough to inspire cooperation.

103. Have a standing rule that there is no breakfast before they are dressed.

Liz finds this is good incentive for her kids. It works well in our house, too, but our eight-year-old is always looking for a way around it. Since "come to the table dressed by 7:15" is our rule, if she gets up early, eats in her PJ's and is still dressed by 7:15, that's fine with us. (It's even better because she has already eaten.)

104. Buy an apron.

I recommend the kind that covers the top and bottom, so when the baby spits at you or the orange juice spurts out, you don't have to rush and change.

105. Put your child to sleep in her clothes for the next day.

Hope finds this very useful for those occasional early meetings when she knows she will be extra rushed. All she has to do in the morning is change her baby's diapers and go. Lynn takes this one step farther. Two-year-old Daniel does not like blankets so at night Lynn dresses him in sweats and a shirt with a blanket sleeper over. She gets him up and gives him breakfast and then peels off the sleeper (with the remains of breakfast on it), changes his diaper and he's all ready to go to child care. For the older child who fights getting dressed, this can cut out the battle. One mom bought several pairs of sweats and the child went right to school in the ones he slept in.

106. Get a good easy-to-care-for haircut.

Gina saves lots of time each and every morning because she got a wash-and-wear haircut.

107. Leave food out for hungry early risers.

If your problem is that the kids get you up too early and you *need* those extra few minutes of sleep, Jane suggests putting out breakfast food. Her four-year-old was thrilled to be able to rummage arround for his own breakfast and take care of himself.

108. Reward your kids for smooth-running mornings.

About once a month, Patti takes the kids out for breakfast at a coffee shop before school to say thank you for harmonious mornings. It's a treat to go out, and everyone brings a book or the newspaper and has a reading breakfast.

109. Keep hairbrushes handy.

Keep a bowl with several hairbrushes, rubber bands, barrettes, etc. near the door so you don't waste time looking for them every morning.

110. Make brushing teeth easy.

Keep a set of toothbrushes in the bathroom near the kitchen (if you have one), or even in the kitchen so the kids don't have far to go to brush their teeth.

111. Buy dental floss holders so the kids can floss their own teeth.

112. Use TV as a reward (not an entitlement).

We do not allow our five-year-old to watch any TV in the morning until she's dressed, eaten, and her teeth are brushed. Then our problem is turning it off when it's time to walk out the door, but at least she's ready. Cynthia suggests turning it off five minutes before you need to leave. Jane suggests taping a show that has 5–15 minute segments and allowing one segment. Evening TV can, of course, be doled out in the same way—not until PJ's are on, teeth brushed, backpack packed, clothes picked out, etc. It's amazing what a little incentive will do to speed up getting ready.

113. Skip morning TV.

Monica does not allow any TV on weekday mornings. She finds that having the TV on makes the kids more hyper and there is always a battle when it is time to leave. Other moms find that a little morning TV offers them a breather to take a shower, put on make-up, or make a quick phone call.

7 ▪ Childcare, School,

& Homework

FINDING QUALITY AFFORDABLE CHILDCARE is one of the biggest problems facing parents today. Whether you are looking for in-home care, family daycare, a childcare center, or after school care, it takes a lot of time and energy. One of the things I find most frustrating is that even when you find a good situation, it doesn't necessarily last a long time. Your child's needs change, your needs change, the provider moves, and you are back to the beginning. I have found, though, that each time I look, I have more confidence, know more what I want and what to look for, and it is easier. Dealing with school and homework is also difficult for working moms. How do you find out what your child is doing in school? How can you be involved when you have so little time? And how do you know that homework is under control? There are no easy answers, but here are a few ideas.

Childcare

114. Choose good childcare at the beginning.

Pat, who is both a mom and a child care center director, reminds us to take your time and look around. Spend time talking to the daycare provider about how she handles everything from feeding to diapering; toilet learning to napping, playing to discipline. It takes a lot of time and energy, but it pays off. You will get a lot more done at work if you are happy with where your kids are. Of course, always be willing to change if it doesn't work out.

115. Choose daycare with pretty long hours (7 am–6 pm or 6:30 am–6:30 pm).

Dale finds this cushion helpful so he doesn't have to walk out on meetings at work. Often family daycare providers are willing to keep your child late occasionally, but it does have to be worked out ahead of time. Providers also will want you to call when you will

be late. Centers have much less flexible hours, so if you anticipate late or early meetings, you should make arrangements for someone else to pick up or take your child.

116. Plan enough time to get to childcare on time.

Make sure there is extra leeway between when your work is supposed to end and when you could actually leave and make it to daycare on time. Kate, a veterinarian, arranged her hours so her day ends at 4:30 but she can leave as late as 5:15 and still make it to pick up her kids. Her job is so demanding that she seldom leaves at 4:30 but always gets out within her extra time. For her, this cuts out the stress of hurrying.

117. Consider in-home care for an infant.

Wendy finds she has less to plan for in advance. You do not have to hurry to get your child dressed, fed and out the door. You do have to have reliable care, though, because if your sitter is late arriving at your house, you will be late to work.

118. For after school care, consider hiring a college student to pick up your kids at school and supervise the afternoon.

He or she can drive to ballet or soccer, help with snacks, homework, and supervise playdates. After several years of after-school programs, Mich hired a male college student to pick up the kids. Anna now goes to ballet and Nathaniel to music. The kids can go home after school and have friends over, and their parents don't have to worry about being on time for pick-up.

119. Hire a preschool teacher or aides for after-school care.

Many preschools and childcare centers have workers that get off at noon or at 3 pm. They are often looking for extra work and they like being around kids.

120. Share after-school care with another family.

Pat found that by sharing a babysitter, her daughter Geneva had a playmate, and she saved money. Of course, whenever you share care, a lot needs to be worked out in advance: whose house? what if someone is sick? what are house rules? what about snacks?

121. Make a trade for after-school care.

Anne has found a solution even cheaper than sharing. She barters a bedroom to a college student in exchange for after-school care. It has worked great.

122. Leave a note for your child.

If your child is coming home before you, try leaving a note with what the child should do before you get home. Include a small chore. This will help her structure the time. Judy suggests always having the child call Mom or Dad at work when she gets home.

123. Get a dog.

If your child comes home alone, get a big dog for security. It makes Markrid feel better and she doesn't even need to give John a key because she doesn't mind leaving the back door unlocked with the dog at home.

124. Make a sick plan.

Before your child gets sick, have a plan. Make a list of 3–5 potential caregivers. This list might include grandparents or other family members if you are lucky, but also think about friends or neighbors who might be willing to watch a sick child occasionally. Contact your local hospital for a list of nursing students who babysit. Your church or synagogue may have retired people who would care for your child. Many communities have babysitting services and nurses registries that can be called with little advance notice. These can be quite expensive but it is good to have back-ups for when you absolutely must get to work. Make your list when your child is well. Ask everyone on the list if she is willing. Think about how you might compensate friends if they don't want to be paid (exchange babysitting, take them out to dinner, etc.) Try out any babysitter ahead of time so you and your child will feel comfortable. This sounds like alot of work (it is), but if you are organized ahead, it really will save a lot of aggravation and juggling when your child gets sick.

125. Be prepared for emergencies.

Schools and daycare centers usually require that you list adults besides you who may be called in an emergency. Nancy suggests sending each friend or relative on the list a medical release form and insurance numbers (you can photocopy the insurance card) so they will have what they need in an emergency.

School

126. Visit your child's classroom at the beginning of the year.

Make the effort to talk to the teacher and get a feel for what's going on. Ask the best way to communicate with the teacher. If she says she is available at school dismissal, explain that you work and would like to know if you can send a note to school, call in the evening, or meet before school. Some teachers will give out their

home phone numbers; some prefer you to send a note and they'll call you back.

127. Work *with* your child's teacher if your child is having problems.

If there is particular stress in the family (separation, illness or death of a family member, moving, job loss), let your child's teacher know so she can help your child. If you travel a lot for work, let the teacher know. Working together, you can make things easier for your child and help her or him do better both at school and at home.

128. Have a regular time when you ask your child about school.

Many moms like the car ride on the way home from after-school care. Children often feel comfortable talking in the car because you watch the road not them while driving. Dinner time is also a good time for everyone to talk about the day's events, but sometimes it is hard for a child to get a word in with everyone talking. I prefer asking the kids either in the car, as soon as I get home, or at bedtime, after lights out. It is nice to have a quiet time with each child individually to talk about how things are going. Often the kids don't want to talk about their day, but I find that if I tell them about mine, they open up. Obviously, it is important to respect a child's privacy, but many children will want to tell you if you show you are a good listener.

129. Volunteer only for school activities that involve your child.

When you are working, it is often hard to be involved with your child's school. Gina suggests not volunteering for school committees, but volunteer for things with the children (field trips, class room time, etc.) so they see your involvement and it doesn't take you away from them in the evenings. Cynthia volunteers one lunch hour a week and reads a story to the class. If you can't volunteer during the day, ask the teacher if there is something you can help with at home in the evening. You and your child can work together sorting papers, etc. The teacher will appreciate your effort, think of you as a fellow worker, and it will probably be easier to talk to her when you need to.

130. Arrange a class field trip to your work.

If your workplace (or one of your business associate's) is interesting to children, arranging a field trip is a great way to contribute to the class. One year I arranged a trip to a printing plant with which I did business. The kids learned a lot and it was fun for all.

Homework

131. If your child has trouble doing homework, he or she needs regular chores.

Margaret is a former math teacher for 5th and 7th grade boys and she found that kids who were having trouble doing homework learned responsibility when they were assigned chores. The homework problems disappeared.

132. Turn off the TV.

Della (and several other moms) suggested that the best way to get homework done is to unplug the television. Connie's rule is "No TV during the week (Monday–Thursday)." This rule is simple to enforce because there are no exceptions. The kids do their homework and the bickering between them over what shows to watch has been eliminated. You might want to try a TV-free week and see if you are fighting less with your kids over homework, chores, and dawdling.

133. Make doing homework a family rule.

Susan handles homework the same way she handles discipline. Eight-year-old Benjamin has had Rules and Consequences since he was three. These are decided each year at a conference around his birthday, and revised during the year as necessary. The Rule is "Do your homework as soon as you get home from school. Period." It's non-negotiable and he knows it. The Consequences are established but vary with the age—no TV, no gold star, etc.

134. Have a set place for your child to do homework.

For some children a desk in their bedroom is ideal for quiet concentration, but others like to be in the midst of family life. Lee put Kira's desk in the den next to hers, so they both work together. My daughter, Leah, likes to work at the kitchen table while I am fixing dinner. It often takes some experimenting to figure out what works the best.

135. Ask about your children's homework.

If you come home late and your children have already finished their homework, you might want to ask if they had any questions or problems. You don't want to become the "homework police" but you do want to make sure they have done it.

8 ∎
Extras

ON THE ONE HAND, you want your kids to have all
the advantages, including ballet, soccer, music lessons,
the list goes on and on. You don't want them to be
deprived because you are working. On the other hand,
you are probably so tired from working and managing
the household, that you just don't want to think about
anything else. One day my husband and I had lunch with
a colleague of his who spent the whole time outlining
their weekend schedule for his two sons. One son played
hockey, both played soccer, and I think one had music as
well. At the end of the recitation of practices, games and
lessons, he turned to us and asked "So what do you do?"
He was appalled that our daughter had *only* ballet *only*
once a week. As far as I could tell, both he and his wife
were hostage to their children's extracurricular

schedules. When you plan their after-school schedules, don't kill yourself trying to do it all; you can't. It really is okay to make life a little easier for you.

Lessons & Activities

136. Let each child choose one thing.

She can choose ballet *or* art class, music *or* soccer—if you even
have the time for that. You don't need to prove you're a supermom
by driving your kids to everything under the sun. One activity at a
time builds commitment and gives you some breathing room.

137. Don't feel guilty about not letting your child do scouts, baseball, or some other time-consuming activity.

Even if another parent thoughtlessly suggests that "every other child in the class does ..." don't let it bother you. It isn't true.

138. Don't do all the driving.

Carpool with other parents at each activity. Or if you simply don't have the time, hire a college kid to drive your child to ballet, or pay another mother on the soccer team to take your child.

139. Take along another child.

If you sign your child up for a Saturday enrichment class or special activity, suggest that your child include a friend or two, and then take the other children. Pat feels this helps her child feel comfortable and it gives another mom some time off.

140. Join or organize a Saturday morning playgroup for your toddler.

It can be very relaxing going to a park with other moms and kids, and it makes you feel you are not missing out on the wonderful mom stuff that stay-at-home moms get. (It may also be a weekly reminder that as "fun" as this is, you like going off to work.) Knowing a group of other moms also offers wonderful support and a chance to discuss diapers, nursery school, food, and all those things that seem mundane but become so absorbing.

141. Organize a family dinner group.

One of Hope's friends is part of a group of four families that rotates houses for dinner every Wednesday or every other Wednesday.

Parties

142. Volunteer first for the easiest thing or something you like.

Judy calls it: "Bring the bread." Instead of waiting for the school committee to assign you stuffed chicken wings, volunteer for something that is easy for you. By volunteering first, you get your choice and your promptness is appreciated.

143. Have your kids make the treats themselves for class parties and bakesales.

144. Buy gifts by mail.

Lesley saves time on family birthday and holiday shopping.

145. Keep a stash of presents on hand.

This eliminates running out on those last minute, time-consuming shopping trips for birthday party presents. Therese keeps a box in the garage with extra gifts. When she finds a good bargain, she buys stuff on sale and saves it. She also buys extra books at the school book fairs and fundraisers to use as gifts. Therese keeps lots of tissue paper and gift bags on hand, so even her youngest can wrap a present easily. She buys the gift bags in large quantities at discount stores when they go on sale.

146. Let your child use her own money to shop while you shop.

Lee finds that buying birthday presents runs more smoothly when her daughter, Kira, brings her allowance and buys something small for herself. This cuts out the begging.

147. **Keep the birthday presents inexpensive.**
Lolita sets a $5 limit on birthday party presents and takes her child to a dollar store to spend the money. Her kids have a terrific time picking out presents.

148. **Have your child open each present as the guest comes in.**
Cynthia finds this makes parties less overwhelming. It gives a special moment with each guest and saves you from the hubbub of all the screaming kids wanting the presents.

149. **For family birthdays, have a "Handy Dandy Birthday Box."**
Just take a big tin (or box with a top) and put all the things you need for birthday celebrations: balloons, candles, crepe paper streamers, signs, decorations, etc. You have all that stuff in one place, and Lolita finds it adds to the excitement when the birthday child can take down the tin and decorate.

150. Don't kill yourself trying to bake the birthday cakes.

You can buy a cake (and not worry about not being a "good mother"). Or you can buy a plain cake and tubes of decorating icing and it is very quick for you or your child to decorate your own cake. Valerie suggests letting the kids make their own. It is fun and they are included in the preparations.

Memories

151. If the thought of keeping up a baby book is overwhelming, have a "baby trunk."

In the trunk Pat stores the baby blanket, artwork, photos (dates on the back), and any trinkets that are special. She plans to put all the stuff in books or whatever when she retires.

152. Sort and save the kids' stuff as you go.

Therese has a system similar to the baby trunk for her four daughters. There is a box for each child, labeled with her name, on the lowest shelf of the linen closet. Therese brings home copy paper boxes from work. (These are strong and have removable lids.) As each child makes something at school or for a holiday, Therese labels it with the date and puts it in the box in the closet. When the box is full, she labels it and moves it out to the garage, and brings home a new box from work. Someday she and the children will sort through all the stuff. She has become judicious about what she saves.

153. Store photos in boxes.

As soon as the pictures come back, date the envelope, add any additional notes, and stop feeling guilty about the photos piling up.

9 ■
Drive Time

DRIVING WITH THE CHILDREN can be so unpleasant you want to scream. There is practically nothing worse at the end of a demanding day at work than to pick up tired, hungry kids and listen to them scream and fight all the way home. On the other hand, car rides can offer a time to actually talk with your children without distractions, a time to listen to music, or just sit and think (and drive). How do you reach the point of having more good car rides that bad ones?

Planning

154. Have snacks in the car ready for your children when you pick them up at school or daycare.

Either pack extra in the lunchbox or have food and a juice box in the car. For me this is a necessity. I have endured many screechy, exhausting, unpleasant rides home. The days the kids have a snack they cheerfully munch and yes, share! I consider car snacks so important on the pick-up that now I will usually stop and get something (yogurt, fruit, bagels) if I've forgotten.

155. Have a small bin or bag of toys and books in the car at all times.

It really keeps toddlers occupied. Therese has her older children bring along books any time they load up for a long ride.

156. Have several "special blankets," and leave one in the car.

If your child can't live without her flannel "B" or fringie, buy several and leave one in the car. When you pick her up at daycare and she forgets it, when you are half way to the sitter's, or when you visit a friend, you won't have to go back to get her special blanket. We once endured an hour of screaming from our three-year-old on a trip. We finally figured out what was wrong, stopped at a mall and bought a new fringed blanket and she immediately calmed down. It was not, of course, exactly the same as the treasured "fringie" but it was good enough. On busy work days the last thing you want to do is lose time by going back or endure the screaming (not to mention wanting your child happy). We have found that three to five of the blankets give enough flexibility so you can wash them.

157. Cut up the favorite blanket into portable pieces.

If your child has only one special blanket and cannot be consoled by any other, Cynthia suggests cutting the treasure into two or four pieces and leaving one in the car.

158. Buy a cassette player with headphones for each child.

Lesley finds this brings peace to car rides. Each child can hear what he wants and the grown-ups don't have to listen. Younger children love the taped stories that go with picture books, and older children like the longer books on tape. Lots of kids love listening to music; it just may not be what you want to hear. This is especially good for long trips.

159. Get tapes you don't mind listening to.

This is a must if you are going to put the kids' tapes on the car tape deck. For toddlers, Hope highly recommends the Discovery Toys tapes with all kinds of noises—violins, doggies, cats, baby crying, man laughing, etc.

160. Buy some relaxing tapes to play on the drive home from work.

Lee reports that it helps with the transition.

161. Train your kids to like what you like.

Cynthia likes oldies. She's trained her kids to like the oldies station by offering valuable prizes when they recognize favorite songs or recording artists. 10¢ for the Beatles, 25¢ for the Four Tops... is a great way to keep the radio on a station you like and have fun with your kids. Try this with classical, jazz, or whatever music *you* like.

162. Use drive time to tell stories.

Every day, sometimes twice a day, Holly tells the kids stories that she thinks up on the spur of the moment.

163. Keep a book in the car for *you.*

When you get to the store and your baby or toddler has fallen asleep and you don't want to wake him, at least you can relax and read. Hope has read a lot this way.

Behaving

164. Set up drive time rules ahead of time.

Let your children know what the rules are and what the consequences are. I expect my children to wear their seat belts, use indoor voices, keep their hands to themselves, and not distract me when I have to concentrate on the driving. Many parents also have rules about radio use.

165. If your kids squabble through car rides, just calmly pull off the road and stop the car.

Don't say anything, just look out the window, flip through papers in your briefcase, whatever. Pretty soon they will notice you've stopped and question you. Simply say, "when you are quiet, we

will continue." I once did this when I was driving a car full of six-year-olds on a school field trip. Boy, were they suprised. They behaved the rest of the way back to school.

166. Play the "Quiet Game."

Whoever can be quiet the longest wins. Lolita finds that her kids think it is hysterical when she loses.

167. Stop the fighting over who sits where.

Do your kids argue over who gets to sit in the front seat? When the bickering got to be too much, Judy told her kids that for several weeks neither could sit in front. Afterwards they were only allowed in the front seat if they did not argue. The arguments ended.

10·
Errands

EVERYBODY HAS TO DO ERRANDS, and I don't know any parent who enjoys them. My philosphy on errands is to keep them to a minimum. There may be some errands you do that don't even need doing. I used to drop off film to be developed and then a day or two later, pick it up—two errands. Now I use the film mailers. Not only does it save time, but the mailers are cheaper. I also don't worry about forgetting about film I have left off. Other errands can wait until you have several things nearby. And if you have a partner, lots of errands can be shared or rotated.

Use the mail

168. Bank by mail. Get cash at the supermarket.

You can usually have your paycheck direct deposited or you can mail in deposits. Many banks offer automatic electronic payment of regular monthly obligations like mortgage and school tuition. Some employers also offer payroll deductions to pay homeowner's and car insurance, or to make automatic deposits to a credit union. For Lesley, this saves time and money (because the insurance is cheaper through her husband's employer) and she doesn't have to worry about forgeting to pay. Most supermarkets allow you a courtesy card to cash checks (often up to $100) over your purchase. This really saves time. In a pinch I'll go to our ATM machine, but never stand in line at the bank.

169. Order stamped envelopes through the mail directly from the post office.

Kate finds this saves time waiting in line at the post office and licking stamps.

170. Shop by catalogue.

Lots of things can be bought by mail which saves time and often money. Ask your friends to pass along catalogues they like. There are also several good books which list mail order companies. Just write for the catalogues that interest you. I like the book *Wholesale By Mail Catalog* (available at bookstores). I have bought several things from companies listed there.

Save time & energy

171. Don't waste time and gas driving distances to stores that are just a little cheaper.

172. Find places to do errands close to childcare.

If you have a little time after work, before your child needs to be picked up, you can do errands without the children along. If the grocery store, drycleaners, or post office is close to where your children are, you can judge your time better.

173. Squeeze short errands in on the way home.

If you don't have time before you pick up the kids, do a quick one after. Or better yet, have your husband do errands while you pick up the kids, or you do errands while he picks them up.

174. Use drive-thru windows.

Banks, fast food, some cleaners, and even some convenience stores have drive-thru service. Toni banks at the drive-thru window so she doesn't have to get the kids out of the car.

175. When you take your kids for a haircut, have them cut yours, too.

Gina finds that this saves lots of money and time. (The kids' haircutters are often cheaper and very good.)

176. Older children can help with errands.

This tip requires having a responsible child over 16, but it worked wonderfully for Judy. When Selene turned 16, her parents gave her a car and paid for the insurance, maintenance, etc. In return for having the use of her own car, Selene was responsible for picking up her younger sister, Lori, from school and driving her to routine things like sports practice. Other things were negotiable, but Selene was expected to help out with some of the other errands. Selene was not expected to be a full time chauffeur for her sister, but she had a regular schedule of responsibilities. All at once, Judy went from having to coordinate schedules and drive two children (as well as work), to having both children be fairly independent. Judy feels that a bit of blackmail is okay with something big like a car, so in addition to being responsible for daily driving for herself and her sister, Selene had to promise to continue her religious education.

Groceries

177. Organize your grocery list so others can shop, too.

Grocery shopping is one of those things that has to be done every week, and somehow, it seems, it always has to be you because you know what's needed and what to buy. Right? Not necessarily. Penny has put her total master grocery list of everything she uses regularly on her computer. She has organized it by aisles at her market. Every week she takes a printout of the list and leaves it out. Anyone can check or circle what is needed. At the end there is blank space for other things that people want. Since the list is usually pretty complete and it is organized like the market, anyone can take the list and do the shopping. Penny admitted it was a big job to get it all written down, but she feels it was definitely worth it. Patricia also makes a master shopping list. She leaves a highlighter pen nearby and it just takes a moment to mark what's needed. She organizes her list by category—dairy, vegetables, cleaning, etc. rather than by grocery aisle. If you don't have a computer, you can write out and organize a master list. Just make copies for weekly use.

178. Put the list on the refrigerator with a pencil.

This is a lot simpler, but it works for Lesley. Whoever finds something is low or gone needs to add it to the list.

179. Annotate the grocery list with size and brand information.

This enables Wendy's husband to do the shopping, too.

180. Enlist your children's help.

Anne gets help with the grocery shopping from her 13-year-old son. Kevin is always looking for extra money, so he clips food coupons, goes to the store with Anne and collects those items. He gets to keep the savings. The coupons must be for items they use and are on the list for the week. Kevin earns extra money and learns about the family shopping; Anne gets help at the market.

181. Don't leave the shopping for the weekend.

Monica finds that even though she is tired by the end of the week, she does her grocery shopping on Friday afternoon to leave the whole weekend free for relaxation and family activities.

182. Cut out the grocery store begging.

Do your kids beg for stuff at the grocery store? You might want to try giving them a weekly allowance and telling them if they want something they can pay for it themselves. Therese has found that as her children learn the value of money (and are spending their own), they lose interest in the junk and stop bugging her.

Stock up

183. Buy in large quantities.

If you have a basement, garage, or other storage space, you can buy nonperishables in huge quantities. Buying toilet paper by the case means you don't have to worry about it for months and months.

184. Stock up on school supplies.

Connie buys stocks of certain school supplies—poster board, report covers, etc., the things they demand at 9 o'clock the night before a project is due.

11 ∎
Evening

THERE ARE JUST NOT ENOUGH HOURS in the evening to have a nice dinner, give the kids a bath, make sure they've done their homework, watch the news, have a lovely bedtime ritual, prepare for the next day, and have enough uninterrupted adult time to return phone calls, get some work done and watch a movie on TV. It is important for everyone to have some relaxing time, but it is not necessary (or I think possible) to do everything every night. You can't skip dinner, but you can make it simple. You can't skip homework, but you can skip bath time. I think the key is deciding on what is necessary, and then how you can schedule in some fun time for the

kids and for yourself. Some nights it seems that the key is just surviving until you can go to bed, but it is really nice when you can look forward to the evening, to having time to read a book or watch a favorite TV show.

Coming home

185. Give your children some attention when you first come home.

Jayne has found that if she gives her daughter the first ten minutes when they come home, the rest of the evening goes much more smoothly. That means, don't try to listen while you are opening the mail or while you are cooking dinner. Stop. Pay attention to your child. Attend to her needs first. This is often very difficult when you are tired, hungry, and still thinking about your work day, but the Moms who do this say it really pays off.

186. Or take care of your personal needs first.

Other moms find that attending to their own needs first gives them renewed energy for dealing with the children. Adele found that she needed a little time alone after coming home from work (to take off her coat, go to the bathroom, check the mail), so she told her school-age children she would be available after ten minutes. After ten minutes she turned her full attention to them to hear about their day. This probably won't work for preschoolers, but older children can be accomodating when they know their needs will be met very soon.

187. Change clothes when you get home.

When Kira was a preschooler, Lee would change into her robe and slippers as soon as she got home. Kira felt secure that Lee would be home for the evening, and Lee didn't have to cuddle in her heels, nylons and suit.

188. Give your child a bath as soon as you get home.

For those days that her daughter whined all the way home, Micki found that putting her in the tub as soon as they got home really helped. The child relaxes and enjoys the bath while you have a few minutes to catch your breath and open the mail. (The child obviously has to be old enough to be in the bath alone.)

189. Take a bath with your toddler.

When Hope comes home really tired, she takes a bath with two-year-old Michael. He gets to play and have Mom-time and she gets to rest and relax in the bath.

190. Have a family group hug when everyone comes home.

It helps Lynn's toddler reconnect with Mom and Dad.

191. Occupy your kids with an art project box.

For that time from 5-7pm when the kids are cranky and parents exhausted, Marlene has an art project box. The big box has yarn, feathers (collected at the park), shells, construction paper, glue, scissors, greeting cards, and whatever else she has saved. When Marlene pulls out the box, the kids can stay occupied for half an hour or more at a time.

Bedtime routine

192. Skip the daily bath (and daily fight over it).

Susan only insists on a bath if her son really needs it. So he is a little dirty. Washing hands, face, neck, and teeth are pretty good for those "off" nights if he isn't too stinky, especially in cooler weather.

193. Put a chair in the bathroom.

Pat has found that a cheap vinyl bean bag chair in the bathroom gives her a comfortable and waterproof place to sit while watching her toddler in the bath. She adds candles, soft music and a book, and even enjoys a relaxing time.

194. Make bathtime fun.

For young children, baths can be more fun when there is something the child can wash, too. Monica suggests large plastic dinosaurs, boats, trucks, and dolls. A net bag or plastic bin to keep and drain the bath toys can be kept in the bathroom, and part of ending the bath routine can be having the child help store the toys.

195. Don't let the telephone interrupt your story or bedtime routine with your child.

Put on your answering machine, or tell whomever calls, you will return the call later. Your child will know she is more important than work or socializing, and bedtime will run more smoothly without interruptions. This is one I have had to force myself to do, but it really pays off. We have a much more relaxed and enjoyable time when I don't jump up to answer the phone. (The machine does a perfectly good job of it!)

196. Put a dimmer on the overhead lights in the kids' rooms.

Judy found that after the bedtime routine (story, chat and kiss) she could dim the lights and let her daughter play on her bed for a few minutes before lights out. The transition helped her quiet down.

197. Try allowing your child to be awake in the bedroom but not allowed to leave the room.

Lee has found this helps when she has a problem getting Kira to bed. Older children can read; pre-readers can look at book or do a puzzle on the bed.

12 ∎
Chores

SOMEONE HAS TO DO THE LAUNDRY, wash the dishes, feed the dog, clean the bathroom, sweep the floor, empty the trash and vacuum the rug. There is no good reason why you have to do it all. If you have a partner, divide up the chores. Have the children do their share. Even very young children can help. While it often seems like having them "help" is really a hindrance, it builds good habits. I find that dividing up chores is one of the most stressful parts of being married and having a family. No one *wants* to do them, everyone realizes they have to be done, but it sure is easier to let things slide by and have someone else pick up the slack. One of the things I have learned is that it helps to be very clear. It is much easier for my husband to know that he is responsible for the laundry, than to come home every night and figure out what needs doing and who should do it. In talking to parents for this book, one of the biggest issues was should kids be paid for doing chores, or should chores be part of family responsibilities? Should you give an allowance? or should allowance be tied to doing chores? Families resolve these issues differently, and I have included several different families' solutions. You and your partner can decide what is best for your family.

Getting help

198. Start by assigning an easy chore.

Despair is the word that best describes how many moms speak about chores. Several said it is easier and quicker to just do the chores themselves rather than get the kids to do anything. Most regret it, though. If your kids don't do anything, start small and stick to it. A regular small chore like sponging off the table after dinner can go a long way towards building responsibility. Even a very small child can clear his own plate from the table. Chores can be tied to TV privileges or other incentives.

199. Start chores young.

Kate is emphatic about making sure children pitch in. Even a two-year-old can sort silverware and place it in the drawer. Nancy says that even her three-year-old can "help." When she is changing the sheets, she lets her daughter play parachute with them and then help her. She also has her daughter help put the clothes in the dryer. In addition to building the habit of helping with chores, it's great for counting and learning colors. Cally also has her two-year-old follow her from the hamper to the washer to pick up anything she drops. Monica reports that she can always get her kids to wash the windows (first floor, of course). It's great water play.

200. Have a family meeting to get chores started or to add new chores.

Jane sat down with five-and-a-half-year-old Mike, discussed that everyone in the family helps do the family jobs, and asked what he would be able and willing to do every day. He said he could clear his plate from the table, so that's what he does. He recently added making his bed and straightening up his room, because he can actually do those things now. Before you have this kind of discussion with your child, I suggest having a list in your mind of suggestions in case your child has no thoughts on what he could do. I also think you should make it clear that he must do something, that "I can't do anything," is not an acceptable response.

201. Allow the children to choose their own jobs.

In Sheila's family the children choose on the condition that they ask Mom and Dad what must be done to contribute to the family's well-being. Everyone hates laundry, so sometimes just for variety, they do each other's.

202. Give your kids a choice of chores.

Anne gives her kids a choice: "Do you want to fold laundry or vacuum?", "Clean the bathroom or the kitchen?" It works.

203. Don't get caught up in the kids' complaints "That's not fair."

Life isn't always fair, but responsibilities do even out. Make an effort to even them out but it isn't always possible.

204. Set a deadline for getting chores done.

Anne always says, "by noon," or "before you can go to your friend's house," or "before you go to bed." The children then know exactly what is expected of them—and they do it.

205. Pick a time that the whole family cleans up together.

Saturday morning is usually a good time. Turn on some energetic music, and finish up with a treat.

206. If your kids complain, make them do it themselves.

Judy told me that since her children were about twelve, if they complained about anything from lunches to laundry, she had them do it themselves. I have tried this with my eight-year-old, and the complaining stops quickly.

207. If dividing up the chores is a problem, Saturday morning post a master chore list.

Each child must do five jobs from the list, and the earlybird chooses. Patti has found this makes eager workers.

208. List Mom and Dad on your chore chart.

Pat suggests that if you do a chore chart, include Mom and Dad and their regular responsibilities, ie. "cook dinner, mow lawn, shopping," This lets the kids see their parents' contributions and stops the incredibly annoying "I have to do everything," from the kids.

209. Give each child a detailed list of responsibilities.

On Saturday morning give each child a list of the responsibilities (don't use the word chores) expected. Be very specific, ie. practice piano, workbook pages, empty wastebasket. This list is like a contract; the child knows everything has to be done that day. If the child is invited out or something comes up, she can reschedule the responsibilities for Sunday, but she knows there are no privileges on Sunday until the list is completed. Emily finds she gets better cooperation because the list doesn't nag. Daughters Meagan and Katie take responsibility for what needs to be done. Emily suggests starting very young; before the children can read, you can make a picture list.

210. Try a chore chart with a reward.

Lisa has a chart in each child's room that lists all the things they are supposed to. They get a check mark for each thing. If they do four things a day they get a star, and if they get a star every day they get their allowance.

211. Reward taking responsibility for chores.

Pat suggests that if you give an allowance, tie it to chores, but have the rates vary with how much responsibility is taken for the chores. For example, chores done without a reminder might be worth $1.00, with a reminder $.50, and chores neglected and done by someone else would require payment of a dollar to that person. This requires having a chore list with times the chores must be completed so the children know when they can take over each others chores or when they must pay out.

212. Try paying your child for housework.

Judy pays nine-year-old Austin for housework. It gives her an income she has to work for. Each job is worth a set amount. Since she is always saving for a toy of some sort, motivation is usually not a problem. Judy likes this approach because housework should be considered monetarily valuable.

213. Put your kids on salary (if they do the work).

Therese's system uses the work world as its model. Mom and Dad work for money and the children (ages 9, 7 ,5, 3), except for the youngest, operate under the same set of rules. Each child has jobs that are listed on a clipboard. If she does her chores, she gets a set amount of money. Bonuses are used as an incentive and can be earned by doing extra chores, having a cheerful attitude, whatever you want to encourage. Once a week, the family has payday and everyone gets paid. If a kid has broken any family rules (which are posted), fines are subtracted from her earnings.

214. Set rules for chore trading.

Do you think kids should be able to swap chores? Emily's solution to this sometimes thorny problem is that the kids can trade, but the chore is still the responsibility of the child to whom it was assigned.

215. Get someone to help clean your house.

If you can afford even a few hours every other week, it helps. The family has to pick up before the cleaner arrives and it motivates everyone. Micheline shared that tip, and I decided to try it in my own house, and it is great. I have just hired someone for three hours every other Thursday, and we managed to have people over a week after she'd cleaned without the usual massive clean-up. Getting some help does not preclude having everyone pitch in. There is always plenty that needs doing.

216. Some chores can be eliminated.

Who ends up setting the table in your house? Valerie has solved that problem, often a battle, by putting the silverware in a pretty basket on the table. Whenever anyone needs it they just take it. It is there all the time.

217. Make chores fun when possible.

For preschoolers, Sheila suggests making setting the table a bit of a game—count the forks, plates, and cups. Liz has found the kids *like* to set the table when they know it means dinner will be served more quickly. Cally lets her two-year-old have water play in the kitchen sink using whatever plastic stuff needs rinsing. If you have wood floors, Ted suggests buying a 3' wide industrial dust mop. Children love swooshing this around, and cleaning the floors becomes very quick.

Picking up

218. Use bins to organize toys.

Is getting the kids to pick up their toys a huge battle? or picking them up yourself a boring waste of time? Leslie suggest sorting the toys into bins, and allowing only one bin out at a time until the kids learn to pick up themselves. Even toddlers can pick up this way and build good habits.

219. Set a consequence for not picking up.
Anne's sister has a basket and any toys, clothes, etc. that she has to pick up goes in the basket. Her kids have to do a chore to get it back.

220. Have the kids pay the maid.
If your children leave their things all over the house and refuse to pick up after themselves, try having them pay the maid (Mom) out of their allowances. Charge for picking up lunch boxes, putting dirty clothes in the hamper, etc. Patti reports that this makes the kids much more conscious of their belongings, and much more willing to pick up.

221. Decide where things are going to be kept and let everyone know.
Make it each person's responsibility to put things back where they belong. This saves Lesley time as her kids don't have to keep asking "Where's the ...?"

222. Keep track of the scissors.
Cynthia suggests putting scissors and scotch tape in the silverware drawer and whoever uses them has to put a dollar (or a toy) in the drawer. It's a reminder to return the scissors. When the scissors are returned they get the dollar back. Several people did not like this idea at all, they felt it was too mercenary, but it works for Cynthia.

223. Buy a shoebag for the hats and gloves.
It keeps them off the floor.

224. Put a small bureau near the outside door.
Adele gave each family member a drawer for hats, mittens, and anything else.

225. Develop cleaning habits over time.
Getting kids to clean their rooms can be a huge battle. Lee suggests that when they are little and just learning about responsibility, they often would prefer to clean something other than their room. Let them do it, praise their initiative and set an example by cleaning up your own room. They will quickly catch on.

Laundry

226. Give the kids their own hamper in their room and make them bring their own laundry to the laundryroom and sort it.
Susan wanted her sons, ages 8 and 12, to do their own laundry. That didn't work so well, but they manage to bring the laundry to the laundryroom and sort it.

227. Wash clothes in bulk once a week or every other week.
You have to have enough clothes for everyone to last, but you don't have to worry about laundry all the time.

228. Have kids put away their own laundry.

Kate sorts it in her bedroom and seven-year-old Erika picks up what is hers. I have recently started putting a basket of sorted folded laundry in each child's room and even five-year-old Allison can put her own things away.

13 ■
Family Time

WITH EVERYONE SO BUSY with things that *have* to be done, it's the things we *want* to do that get the short end. It can be discouraging when you go to a lot of effort to plan an activity and it just isn't fun. This spring we planned a lovely five day family trip to a lake with our two kids and a dog, and it turned out terrible. The kids complained they didn't have anyone to play with, the resort cabin which sounded good in the brochure was tiny and not so pretty, and the altitude bothered everyone. Sometimes smaller, spur of the moment activities have worked better. A few weeks ago we

rented a video movie and all sat on our bed enjoying it thoroughly. Last Friday my husband and I decided at the last minute to pick the kids up at camp and go out to dinner. It was great fun. As the kids get older, it seems harder to claim their time and attention for family activities, but I think it is just as important. Having time together as a family is what makes all this running around worthwhile. If you are not in the habit of doing things as a family, I would start small and see how it goes. Be persistent, though, and the time and energy invested will pay off.

Anytime

229. Make breakfast the family meal.

Get up early and make a nice breakfast. Sit with the kids and talk while they eat pancakes, oatmeal, eggs, etc. Della finds that with her long hours and erratic schedule, having breakfast together is the only family time she can be sure of, and it starts the day off right. This also works well as the kids get older and their schedules of play rehearsals, sports events, and babysitting jobs interfere with family dinner.

230. Establish family fun time.

Pick some time on the weekend that everyone can be free to do family outings and then plan some things you've been meaning to do. Be flexible about birthday parties and invitations, but plan some fun time with the family.

231. Watch TV together.

Some families enjoy choosing a television show to watch together every week and order in pizza. When I was growing up, Sunday nights the whole family watched "College Bowl" and answered the questions. Liz suggests learning to like something the kids like. She enjoys the reruns of "Rocky & Bullwinkle" with her kids.

232. Even if you do not like what the kids watch on TV, watch with them occasionally.

It gives you an opportunity to express your views on certain subjects and give concrete reasons about what you approve or disapprove of in a program. The television show they like can also be a good conversation starter and lead to good family discussions.

233. Rent a family video and all watch together.

It's cheaper than a trip to the movies. Some public libraries even lend videos for free.

234. Try the library storytime.

Lisa suggests that the Saturday morning storytime at her local library is an excellent regular family time.

235. If you are lucky enough to live near a beach (ocean, lake, river) use it.

Going to the beach is one of the few family activities that pleases all age groups. We can read or talk while the kids play. Anne, who has kids ranging from 5 to 15 finds that the beach has something for everyone. Bring sandwiches, drinks and snacks and stay for lunch or supper. If the thought of organizing a picnic is too much trouble, buy sandwiches on the way. Invite another family along and your kids will have company. It's amazing how relaxing a family outing can be.

236. Eat out together—but request a booth.

When Cally and her husband take their two-year-old daughter out to dinner, they always request a booth. It gives children a little more room for coloring, eating, and stretching, and you don't have to watch them quite so closely.

237. Stick with family restaurants.

After several dining disasters with young children at adult restaurants, Monica has settled on two or three family restaurants. One provides crayons and coloring pages; another has a soup and salad bar that has so many choices it satisfies even the pickiest eater. Liz likes to choose a restaurant with an outside dining area (obviously not possible in the winter in the north). The kids are more relaxed, they can move around and people seem more tolerant outside.

238. Bring something to do to restaurants.

Marilyn always brings coloring books and a bag of crayons when she takes the kids to a restaurant. My eight-year-old daughter, Leah, brings her reading book with her when we go to a restaurant and that has helped a lot.

239. Have a regular Game Night at home.

Teach the kids card games and board games as soon as possible. Invite another family over and ask them to bring their favorite game. Lee finds it is a good way to make family friends.

240. Don't schedule Saturday morning sports and lessons.

Spend early Saturday morning snuggling, telling stories, and having breakfast together. With all the pressure to do more, this one isn't so easy, but can really pay off in a more relaxed weekend.

241. Get the kids out early on Saturday morning.

Dale finds they have lots of fun and are much more interested and energetic the whole day.

242. If you don't have room for a sandbox, fill up a wheelbarrow with sand.

Cally finds it's perfect for toddlers and preschoolers because they can stand and play. You can move it around the yard so you can get yard work done while the kids play nearby.

Vacations

243. Plan short vacations, like long weekends.

When the kids are small, it doesn't matter if they miss a day or two of school, and a short trip can boost everyone's spirits.

244. Plan a trip with another family.

It gives the kids playmates, and the adults grown-up social time and a chance to split up and not be on duty every second. Our best vacations have been when we have rented a house at the beach, lake or mountains with another family, or gone camping with one or more families.

245. Bring a teenager along on a trip to help you with the kids.

One of the things we realized about so-called vacations, is that they are more work than staying home. At home we had school and daycare to help out, but on vacation watching the kids was constant. A few summers ago we brought along an eighth grade babysitter when we went camping and it was great. She read to the kids, helped get them ready for bed, and played with them so we could have some reading time.

246. Plan trips with relatives carefully.

If you are visiting relatives, think beforehand about how their household runs and how you can accomodate your family's needs. If they don't eat between meals and your kids do, bring your own set of snacks. To avoid unpleasantness, talk to your relatives beforehand about your family's routine. Obviously, you can't go into someone's home and dictate how it runs, but if you talk things over you can come to agreements. If your kids are used to eating at 6 and your parents eat at 7 (and don't want to try an early dinner), you can decide on either a healthy early snack, or feeding the children early and the grown-ups later. Don't wait until the kids are screaming because they are expecting dinner, and your mother is wondering out loud why the children have no manners.

247. Try a vacation at one of the resorts or family camps that have special kids' activities.

You can have fun together, but also have some grown-up time.

14∎
Work

MOST OF THE WORKING MOMS I KNOW like to
work and want to work, they just wish they could cut
down on the stress of balancing conflicting demands.
Added pressure sometimes comes from an anti-family
feeling in the workplace, and the need to prove that
parenthood doesn't interfere with working. In the midst
of all the stress, we feel guilty about working too much,
guilty about not working enough, guilty that the kids
aren't getting enough. It's time to give ourselves a break
and not feel guilty about combining work and family.
Many moms find a solution in working less; others in

rearranging schedules. For the moms who don't have
much control over their work schedules, exerting more
control in other areas (like finding terrific childcare and
delegating household chores) helps keep their sanity.
Most working moms like that their children see them as
workers, not just as someone to cater to their needs.

Scheduling

248. Lots of Moms said work part-time or job-share.

In many jobs you can arrange to work three days a week, just mornings, or one week on one off. You gain flexibility but probably lose out on benefits and promotions. It is a very tough choice but it seems to work for more and more moms I talked to.

249. Experiment with flexible hours.

Many moms can't afford to work part time, and many jobs won't allow it, but many offer flexible hours and that can really help. Judy found that leaving work early on Tuesday and taking her daughters to piano and gymnastics helped her to feel involved with them. By staying late and making up those hours on Friday afternoon, the work got done and the children had special regular time with their Dad, too. She also did not have to end a tiring work week with cooking dinner.

250. Negotiate your own schedule.

Lynn talked to her supervisor and was able to adjust her work schedule so she arrives at work *very* early (6:30 am) and then can leave earlier. She is able to spend more time with the children in the afternoon and evening, can schedule doctor's appointments, and do errands. She finds that unfortunately the time fills up with sports for the kids and errands, but holding the line on after school activities is another issue. Liz has also arranged her schedule to work early and lets a sitter have the early morning hassles of grumpy kids. She gets off early and has the after-school fun.

251. Arrange a midweek day off.

Pat suggests working four ten-hour days. She finds that taking Wednesday off is great. On Sunday she only has to get organized for two days, and on Wednesday the same. Three day weekends sound nice, but having Wednesday off really gives her a break.

252. Coordinate work hours with your partner.

In addition to changing to an earlier schedule (7:30 am–4 pm), Wendy and her husband stagger their hours. He doesn't start work until 9 or 9:15 and comes home about 6:15 pm. This way, their son is with a babysitter for less time each day and both mom and dad get some special individual time with him.

253. Take a shorter lunch break at work if it enables you to leave earlier.

Lynn seldom takes a true lunch break, and this makes up for her not working weekends. With management approval, other of her co-workers have trimmed their lunch breaks to 1/2 an hour and leave early (or get in late).

Changing

254. Work for yourself.

Marie left a corporate job and is using her skills to build her own business. She admits that the hours can be longer, but there is a lot more flexibility and she feels much more in control.

255. Work at home.

Susan, who also works for herself, finds that working at home saves her a lot of time. She doesn't have to commute and she doesn't waste time in endless meetings with colleagues. Working at home, of course, is not for everyone. It can be hard to discipline yourself to get started each day, it can be lonely, and the refrigerator is always there to tempt you. It is worth considering though. Sometimes it is possible to arrange with your employer to work out of home one or two days a week and go into the office the other days.

Work & family

256. Do errands on your lunch hour.

Then you don't have to do them on the weekends. Or take your lunch hour for *you*! Liz suggests a nice lunch, a walk, some shopping for you. Lunch hour can be a good breathing space between the seemingly constant demands of work and family.

257. Bring your child to the office now and then.

Jayne recommends an office visit about once a year for half a day or a day. Your child gets to see where you work and what you do. That helps your child place you in a context while you are gone. The office people also get to meet your child, so when she calls they can be more personal.

258. Talk to other parents at work.

Develop a community with similar concerns. This can be an informal group of parents you know, or a more organized company parent group. This may not result in immediate policy changes, but at least parenting concerns will not be viewed as your own personal problem.

259. Share the responsibility of doctor's appointments and sick childcare with your partner.

Your partner may be in the habit of assuming that if someone needs to take time off from work it is you. Speak up. Discuss your work needs together.

260. Talk about work with your kids.

Lee shared that there are some wonderful books for children on mothers at work that show mothers doing a variety of jobs. Show these to your children when they are young, and it will seem normal (as it is) that mom works. They'll respect and emulate you.

15·
Exercise

GETTING EXERCISE HELPS YOU keep healthy and makes you feel better. While exercise is often the first thing to be cut when the schedule gets tight, it is important to try and squeeze it in. I know that when I don't get exercise, I get more tired, hungrier and crankier.

Without kids

261. Work out a time with your partner when each of you will exercise, then stick to it.

Jennie goes to a class twice a week—even if she doesn't feel like it. The family accepts it and expects it, and adhering to the schedule helps Jennie's state of mind.

262. Try early morning exercise.

When Leah was a baby, I went running very early in the morning. My husband got her up and fed, so not only did I get some exercise, but I had a break in responsibiliies. And they got some special time together.

263. Take your baby to exercise class.

Lee found she could take her infant to exercise class and put her on a blanket. The baby liked to watch and it was fun for Mom. This worked for about half a year.

264. Take your older child, too.

Margaret goes to aerobics three times a week. Doesn't that sound great? Eight-year-old Philip brings a book, homework, or a toy to amuse himself. Margaret tells him: "If I have to sit through soccer and Little League, you can sit through aerobics."

265. Join a gym that has childcare.

Many gyms offer childcare for the time you are in a class or working the machines. Call around and see if there is one near you. Often they advertise in local parenting newspapers.

266. Walk the dog.

I have found this is a good way to get out of the house. Either early
in the morning (6:30 am) or after the kids are in bed, I take the dog
out walking with a neighborhood friend. It is social and I get
exercise. Lee suggests taking the children along. It teaches
responsibility for your pet along while offering some together-
time.

267. Investigate work sponsored athletic programs.

Many offices offer opportunities for exercise, from pickup basketball games and loosely organized walking clubs to highly competitive team sports. Ask around at work. It never hurts to try.

268. Buy a piece of exercise eqipment (stationary bike, rowing machine, treadmill, etc.) and use it.

Make yourself exercise while you watch the news.

With the kids

269. Sign the kids up for swim lessons at a time you can swim laps.

I tried this last winter and it was great. Monday and Wednesday from 4:30–5 pm the kids had lessons and I swam laps. One year when Leah had ballet on Saturday morning I took a grown-up jazz dance class at the same time. Judy suggests a belly dancing class as great exercise.

270. Swim laps while your kids play in the pool.

When your kids swim well enough so you feel they are water safe, you can swim laps while they swim and play in the pool. For my five-year-old I have a rule that she cannot go beyond the 5 foot mark. It took only one time-out on the side of the pool (while all the other kids kept swimming) for her to learn and keep to her boundaries.

271. Family volleyball games are a fun way to combine exercise and family time.

272. Walk with your child.

When your child is old enough to really walk or run, you can actually schedule in a walk time with the child. She can even ride a bike while you walk or jog. Some moms find it is great to start the day with an early walk with their child.

273. When your child is small take your child in a bicycle seat.

274. Ride bikes together.

As the kids learn to ride better, you can ride with them. For Liz, this combines family time, fun time, and exercise. The kids may not be able to go as fast or as far as you would like, but it is better than nothing.

275. Jog while the kids play.

When her kids were small, Judy took them to the park and jogged small laps around the play equipment. She got exercise while her kids played, and she could easily watch them.

16.
Grown-up Time

WHEN IS THE LAST TIME you went to a movie? Had a romantic evening with your partner? Went out to dinner with friends (no kids)? Or read a novel? If you can't remember, chances are you have neglected grown-up time. You probably are so busy making sure you've done everything for work and for the kids that you haven't thought much about yourself. It really is okay to let a few things slide so you can so some things for yourself.

Going out

276. Get a babysitter.

It is not as hard as you might think. Ask your friends who they use. Some people are reluctant to share sitters, but others don't mind. Ask at your child's school if any of the older children babysit. Walk up and down your neighborhood and talk to the teenagers outside playing. Ask your friends for the going rate, and make sure you agree on a price before you engage a sitter. As you would expect, college kids charge more than high school kids who charge more than Jr. High sitters. Many people use a range of sitters—younger ones when they are just going out to dinner close by and older ones for longer daytime periods. It helps to have a list of sitters so when you decide you want to go out, you can feel confident you'll be able to.

277. Plan a regular time out alone without the kids.

Cynthia recommends having a regular Saturday night babysitter. Hope also has a regular Saturday night sitter and goes out even when she doesn't feel like it. She is usually glad once she's out. My husband and I opt for an almost regular Friday afternoon movie date while the kids are at school and the movies are cheaper and less crowded.

278. If you have an evening babysitter, make sure she puts the kids to bed.

It is no fun to come home from dinner or a movie and hassle over bedtime. Judy and her husband used to drive away from the house and go out again if they saw the kids' lights were still on.

279. Have the babysitter come early.

Does the thought of showering, changing, and getting the kids fed and ready almost make you want to forget about getting a sitter and going out? Ask the baby sitter to come early and take care of the kids while you get ready. We have found this often helps the transition because by the time we are ready to go, the kids are involved with the sitter.

280. Join or start a babysitting co-op.

If it is hard to find a babysitter or you don't have the money, try a babysitting co-op. In exchange for caring for other kids (who are playmates for your own), you get free babysitting time with experienced parent sitters.

281. Trade babysitting with a friend.

If joining a babysitting co-op sounds like too much work (and it sure did to me), find a friend and babysit for each other one or two nights a month. Lesley and Lois find this works very well.

282. Cut down your social obligations.

If you eliminate or reduce the *shoulds* you have time for the *wants*. Susan and her husband spend less time socializing but more of it is with people they really want to see.

283. Take a class in anything that interests you.

Choose something that doesn't *add* stress to your life. Connie reports that her husband and kids seem to respect a firmly scheduled class more than any time she tries to create for herself at home. There is also less debate about getting out of the house than with randomly scheduled activities.

284. Organize a regular once a month book group, wine tasting group, dinner club or bowling group.

For years (since way before kids) I've had a monthly women only book group. Rarely will everyone have time to read the book, but we always have time to get together for supper and socializing. For fifteen years, Diane had a monthly Sunday night supper and bridge group with three other couples. Everyone looked forward to it and they even went away on trips together without the children.

285. Schedule time during the work week to see friends for lunch.

Susan even schedules in time for phone chats.

286. Carry a book or a small knitting project with you wherever you go.

There is a lot of waiting time and even small bits can be grabbed. Connie reads mysteries while pumping gas. She carries around a huge purse so she always has something to do.

287. Treat yourself to a massage.

288. Take a vacation with your partner without the children.

If you are a single mom, take a vacation with a friend. My husband and I go away for a night or two every six months and it is great. If you are lucky enough to have relatives eager (or at least willing) to take the kids, it is easier, but it is still possible if you don't. We do not have relatives close by so getting away takes a lot of planning, but it is worth it. We have had Allison's preschool teacher stay at our house with the children, we have had them stay a night with friends, and we have had both of them stay overnight with Allison's former daycare mom. We have found that for the short trips, it is easier to go during the week when the kids have school or daycare, and it's just the evenings we need to coordinate. Longer trips are obviously harder to plan, but often relatives will help, even from far away. We recently took a week vacation for the first time in five-and-a-half years, and the children flew themselves to stay with my parents. Other families have the grandparents come live in their house for a week. Although with all you have to do, the idea of planning even a night away may seem daunting, it is wonderful to have some time alone with your partner. As much as you love your kids, and miss them, the time off is invigorating.

At home

289. Have the babysitter take the kids out of the house so you can have some time at home for yourself.

290. Go off duty regularly.

Are you overwhelmed with being "on call" 24 hours a day? Judy recommends choosing a regular time when you are "off duty." You might say that after 8:30 every night, the kids cannot bother you with "Where's my blue dress?" "I need cookies for a school party tomorrow," etc. They will soon learn to ask for what they need before you go off duty or wait until the morning. Judy has seen this tip work with a friend's very young children, and it works on her own teenagers. Judy makes exceptions for talking with the kids when they come in from a date. And you are, of course, there for emergencies.

291. Schedule in sleep time.

Sleep seems to be what mothers crave the most (at least that is what they mention first and most often). Therefore, have a naptime for *you*. Mich ends up staying up until almost midnight on weeknights, but Saturdays she sleeps in while her husband takes charge. She feels she couldn't survive without her Saturday mornings. If you are a single mom, it's a little harder, but many young children are happy to turn on Saturday morning cartoons themselves while mom sleeps. I prefer Saturday afternoon naptime which was easier when my kids took naps, but I am training them to have a quiet time to let me sleep.

292. Rest before the kids come home.

It is great if you can arrange to get home a few minutes before the kids. Lesley finds that if she lies down for just ten minutes before the kids come in, she feels restored (at least enough to make it through the evening).

293. Choose birth control that does not make you plan sex.

Sex is another subject often joked about by busy working moms. If you listen to the kidding, no one is having any sex at all. My suggestion is to get an IUD. Another Mom suggested a tubal ligation. (Obviously you need to consult with your doctor.) It is amazing what a difference birth control that you don't have to think about makes. I was always "too tired" to put in the diaphragm, but I would say (conservatively) that the IUD has caused a 300% improvement in our sex life.

294. Get a lock for your bedroom door.

Also let the kids know they may not walk in on you in the bathroom.

295. Have a place of your own at home.

Connie has her own room at home, an art studio. The kids can use it "by reservation only" and there is a sign-in sheet. The last person to use it must clean it. My husband has a small study which the kids may not use—it's his space.

296. Move the TV out of your bedroom.

Monica and her husband felt they never had any privacy, especially in the morning. Moving the TV out and putting a lock on their door helped them reclaim their own space.

297. Have a late evening dinner with your partner.

Lee suggests once a week, give the kids dinner early, put them to bed (or tell them you are off duty) and have a nice quiet dinner just the two of you. You can cook something special that is simple, pick up take-out, or order a pizza. If you are a single parent, make yourself a special meal or invite a friend over.

Easy
Do-ahead
Dinners

THIS BOOK DOES NOT PRETEND to be a recipe book, but when I was gathering tips, a few moms considered it critical to have a few easy do-ahead dinners that the children like. I asked them to share their favorites. I have also included my own lasagna recipe which is unbelievably easy. You don't precook the noodles; you don't make your own sauce. There's only one bowl besides the baking dish.

Very Easy Lasagna

1 small container ricotta cheese, 15 oz.
2 eggs
1 tsp. allspice
3/4 tsp. salt
1/4 tsp. pepper
1 box frozen chopped spinach, thawed
1 large jar spagetti sauce, 26 oz.
1 box lasagna noodles, 12 oz., *uncooked*
1 lb. mozzarella cheese, sliced or grated
1/4 cup Parmesan cheese, grated

Beat ricotta, eggs, allspice, salt, and pepper with electric mixer until smooth. Stir in spinach. Spread a little sauce on the bottom of a 9×13 baking dish.Arrange a layer of dry noodles. Spread about 1/3 of ricotta mixture. Cover with mozzarella. spread a layer of sauce. Add two more layers in same way, ending with sauce. Sprinkle with Parmesan. Bake 350° 30 minutes covered, then 15 minutes uncovered.

Mediterranean Beef & Rice

1/2 tsp. garlic powder
1/4 tsp. ground cinnamon
2 cans (14 1/2 oz.) Italian Style stewed tomatoes
1 1/2 cup uncooked rice
1/2 cup raisins
1 lb. lean ground beef or turkey
3/4 cup sliced green onions

In 3 quart saucepan, brown meat; drain. Stir in garlic and cinnamon. Salt and pepper to taste. Drain tomatoes; pour liquid into a measuring cup. Add enough water to measure 2 1/2 cups. Add liquid to saucepan. Bring to a boil. Stir in tomatoes, rice, raisins, and green onions. Cook over medium heat until liquid is absorbed.

Baked Chicken & Rice

1 chicken cut into pieces
1 1/2 cups rice, uncooked
3 cups chicken broth or water or combination
1 can cream of mushroom soup, undiluted
1/2 package of dried onion soup
Paprika (optional)

Butter a casserole dish. Sprinkle rice on bottom. Add broth or water. Place chicken on top of rice; do not overlap. Sprinkle paprika. Sprinkle dried onion soup. Spread can of cream of mushroom soup over all this. Bake at 325° for 1 1/2 hours uncovered, then 1/2 hour covered. After about an hour, check and see if the rice needs more liquid; if it does, add some. It usually doesn't need the whole two hours, so take it out when the rice is done (1 1/2 - 2 hours). My kids absolutely love this and even though it takes a long time cooking it is easy to make and they will eat it for several nights.

Sloppy Joes

1 1/2 cup beef broth
1 tsp. chili powder
1 tsp. ground cumin
Scant 1/4 tsp. cayenne pepper
5 1/2 oz. (2 cups) rotini pasta cooked
1 cup shredded sharp cheddar cheese
1 lb. lean ground turkey or beef
1/2 tsp. salt
1 Tbs. oil, optional
1/2 cup chopped onion
1 large clove garlic, minced
1 medium green pepper, chopped
1 1/2 cup frozen or canned corn (drained)
1 6oz. can Italian seasoned tomato paste

Brown meat with 1/4 tsp. salt, about 3 minutes. remove meat from pan. Drain all but 1Tbs. fat, or add oil as necessary. Cook onion, garlic, and green pepper over medium heat until tender crisp, about 4 minutes. Reduce heat to low. Add corn, tomato paste, beef broth, chili powder, cumin, remaining 1/4 tsp. salt and cayenne. Simmer uncovered about 5 minutes. Remove from heat. Add meat and pasta. Toss to combine. Transfer to baking dish. Bake 350° for 25 minutes, uncovered. Sprinkle with cheese and bake until melted, about 10 minutes.

Noodle Doodle

1 lb. ground beef or turkey
1 onion, chopped
2 stalks celery, sliced
1 big can diced tomatoes
1 lb. short wide egg noodles or bows
1/2 lb. shredded Swiss cheese

Saute meat with chopped onion and celery. Drain the fat. Add the canned tomatoes, noodles, and cheese. Toss. Bake at 350° for 45 minutes.

Broccoli Pasta

1 head fresh broccoli
Garlic
Olive oil
Pasta
Mozzarella cheese, shredded

Cut up the broccoli. Toss in oil in a deep, heavy pan. Add garlic cloves.Cook over medium heat for a few minutes. Add a little liquid. cover pan and simmer until broccoli is soft. Cook pasta. Mash the broccoli. Toss in pasta and mozzarella.

Easy Shepherd's Pie

Potatoes, 3 or 4
Salt
Butter
Milk
1 package frozen peas or beans
1 lb. hamburger

Wash and cut up potatoes. (There's no need to peel them, the skin has a lot of vitamins.) Boil until soft. While the potatoes are cooking, brown the meat. Salt or season to taste. Drain the fat. When the potatoes are done, drain the water. Mash. Add a bit of butter and milk, and keep mashing until the potatoes are the right consitency. Salt to taste. Pour the drained meat into a 9x9 pan. Spread the frozen vegetables on top, and cover with the mashed potatoes. Bake at 350° for about 20 minutes, until the vegetables are hot. You can precook the vegetables in the microwave so the whole thing will be hot sooner. This one is especially pretty in a glass pan (so you can see the layers), and it freezes very well.

Quick Last Minute Suppers

AS ORGANIZED AS I WOULD LIKE TO BE, there are at least one or two nights a week when I come home and don't have the faintest idea what we should have for supper. Since that probably happens to you, too, I thought you might like a few suggestions for suppers you can do in no time flat.

Soup &
Hot Tuna Sandwiches

Heat up any kind of canned soup. Combine tuna with yogurt or mayonaise. Add diced celery, onions or carrots if you wish. I also often add fresh peaches or apples. Arrange bread on baking sheet. Spread tuna mixture on each. Top with a slice of cheese. Sprinkle with paprika. Bake at 350° until cheese is melted. Eat the soup while the sandwiches are cooking.

Instant Burritos

Open a can of refried beans (I like the vegetarian ones the best). Put a few spoonfuls on a flour tortilla. Top with shredded cheese and salsa (optional). If you want, add any leftover rice, corn, or meat. Roll up. Heat in microwave (about 1-2 minutes per burrito).

Chef's Salad

Cut up turkey (I buy the already cooked turkey breast and use it for sandwiches and quick dinners), cheese, and any kind of salad vegetables. Combine with some shredded lettuce. Add dressing. Serve with extra quick garlic toast. Melt a bit of butter in the microwave. Take any kind of bread or rolls and brush with the butter. Sprinkle garlic salt on and toast.

The Total Baked Potato

Bake some potatoes in the microwave. (Every microwave is different, but around 3 or 4 minutes per potato should do it). While they are cooking, cut up some tomatoes, cheese, leftover meat or vegetables, whatever you want. Salsa, sour cream, yogurt, blue cheese or ranch salad dressing are all good on top. My kids love fried hamburger meat in baked potatoes (which is also good on spagetti.) Let the kids assemble their own—they love the choices.

Super Fast Pizza

Pizza can be made out of practically anything. Just keep a jar of spagetti sauce on hand. For the crust, use those premade Bobolli crusts or English muffins, sandwich rolls or even bread. If you use bread, toast it first so it won't get soggy. Spread some spagetti or pizza sauce on the crust and add whatever you like—cheese, chicken, salami, onions, mushrooms, olives, pineapple, pepper. Bake at 450° until the cheese melts. Let the kids assemble their own and they are sure to eat it.

Spagetti Carbonara

This one is good if your kids like spagetti, but you get tired of that red sauce. Cook some spagetti. While it is cooking, break an egg in a serving bowl. Beat with a fork. Add shredded cheese and garlic powder. If you want (if your kids will eat it) add fresh parsely. If you want meat, cut up some salami (quicker than cooking sausage which is also good). Drain cooked spagetti and toss in egg and cheese mixture. The heat from the spagetti will cook the egg and melt the cheese. Salt and pepper to taste.

Spanish Tortilla

This is really a potato omelette. Dice a few potatoes very fine (they cook quickly that way). Cook in a bit of olive oil until tender. Salt to taste. Beat a few eggs with a fork. Pour over potatoes. Cook. When firm, flip and cook on the other side. This is a tasty, filling supper that has been a favorite in our house since the first time I tried it.

Persian Cucumber Salad

This is a good, quick side dish that our kids love. Peel and dice cucumbers. Toss with plain yogurt. Add garlic powder, salt and pepper to taste.

Middle Eastern Salad

Dice tomatoes and peeled cucumbers. Toss with oil and lemon juice. Salt and pepper to taste. Our kids also like this, and it keeps well in the refrigerator.

Further Reading

I know that you barely have time sleep, let alone read, so I thought I would share a very short list of books. I hope you find them helpful.

Discipline

Win the Whining War & Other Skirmishes : A family peace plan by Cynthia Whitham (Perspective Publishing) offers you a step-by-step plan for dealing with whining, tantrums, dawdling, talking back, and all that annoying behavior that drives parents crazy. It will help you increase cooperation and reduce conflict with children ages 2–12 years old. It is easy to use and very effective.

"The Answer is NO": Saying it and sticking to it also by Cynthia Whitham (Perspective Publishing) will help you say "no" when you need to. The author takes about twenty-five situations like bedtime, pets, designer clothes, music, and homework resistance and helps you define your values and apply them to the problem. This book will definitely help if you have trouble setting limits.

Without Spanking or Spoiling by Elizabeth Crary (Parenting Press) is a must if you have a preschooler. The book combines advice on problems with lots of information on what is appropriate for young children ages about 1–6. It is full of examples.

Sleep

Solve your Child's Sleep Problems by Richard Ferber (Simon & Schuster) was one of the few books I actually used. It was a godsend. It is clear and sensible and we followed the plan and got my daughter to sleep.

The Sleep Book for Tired Parents by Rebecca Huntly (Parenting Press) looks at four different ways to help your child get to sleep. So, if you have trouble with Ferber's plan, don't despair, try something else from this book.

Chores & Errands

The Wholesale-by-Mail Catalog by the Print Project (HarperPerennial) will save you tons of time shopping. It gives you information on hundreds of companies that sell quality merchandise by mail, all for prices at least 30% below retail. I have requested catalogues and ordered from several companies listed in the book, and have been thoroughly satisfied.

Pick Up Your Socks... by Elizabeth Crary (Parenting Press) is a practical book for helping you teach your children responsibility. It will help you figure out what your child can do and how to get him to do it.

Is There Life After Housework by Don Aslett (Writer's Digest Books) tells you how to actually clean your house. It helps with techniques, tools, and instructions, and with tips on making things easier. This was recommended by several parents.

Child Development

The Gesell Institute of Child Development puts out a series of books, one for each year of your child's age, *Your Four year-old*, etc. by Louise Bates Ames and Frances L. Ilg (published by Delta, some of the books are authored by Ames and Haber,). Several parents highly recommended these books as guidelines for knowing what to expect of your child developmentally. I find these books alternately informative and frustrating—yes it is interesting to know what most four-year-olds do, but the books are descriptive and don't really help you cope with the behavior.

Take a look at these catalogues for good parenting books:
Children's Small Press Collection 1-800-221-8056
Childswork Childsplay 1-800-962-1141
Parenting Press 1-800-992-6657

More from Perspective Publishing

Perspective Publishing is a small independent publishing company which helps parents with the problems you face every day: discipline, friendship problems, talking with your kids, balancing work and family, challenging and inspiring your kids.

The Guilt-Free Guide to Your New Life as a Mom: Practical ways to take care of yourself, your life & your baby – all the the same time
by Sheryl Gurrentz

Expectant and new moms need help with everything, and this easy-to-use practical book helps new mothers take care of themselves and everything else in their lives while taking care of their babies.

ISBN: 1-930085-01-X; paperback, 6"x9"; 250 pages; $14.95

Win the Whining War & Other Skirmishes: A family peace plan
by Cynthia Whitham, MSW

This easy-to-use guide helps parents increase cooperation and reduce conflict with children ages 2-12. Step-by-step, parents learn how to cut out all the annoying behavior (tantrums, teasing, dawdling, interrupting, complaining, etc.) that drives them crazy.

ISBN: 0-9622036-3-7, paperback. 6"x9"; 208 pages; $13.95

"The Answer is NO": Saying it and sticking to it
by Cynthia Whitham, MSW

Tackling twenty-six situations that plague parents of 2 to 12-year-olds, this book helps parents define their values, build good parenting habits, and set firm, fair limits. Bedtime, pets, makeup, music, TV, homework, and designer clothes are just a few of the problems covered.

ISBN: 0-9622036-4-5, paperback. 6"x9"; 224 pages; $13.95l

Survival Tips for Working Moms: 297 REAL Tips from REAL Moms
by Linda Goodman Pillsbury

Full of examples of how the tips actually work in real families, this is a light but no-nonsense practical resource thast can help every working mom. From chores to childcare, errands to exercise, this book makes life easier. Almost 100 cartoons make this a book you can't put down.

ISBN: 0-9622036-5-3, paperback. 6"x9"; 192 pages; $10.95

Good Friends Are Hard to Find: Help your child find, make and keep friends
by Fred Frankel, Ph.D.

Step-by-step, parents learn to help their 5 to 12-year-olds make friends and solve problems with other kids, including teasing, bullying and meanness. Based on UCLA's world renowned Children's Social Skills Program, this book teaches clinically tested techniques that really work.

ISBN: 0-9622036-7-X, paperback. 6"x9"; 242 pages; $13.95

Before She Gets Her Period:Talking to your daughter about menstruation
by Jessica B. Gillooly, Ph.D.

This friendly book has up-to-date information and uses real personal stories, exercises and activities to help parents talk with their daughters about menstruation — even if their daughters don't want to talk. It's the only book about menstruation written for parents.

ISBN: 0-9622036-9-6, paperback. 6"x9"; 166 pages; $13.95

Order now: 1-800-330-5851 or www.familyhelp.com (more on other side)